Comparative Political Development

The Precedent of the West

Comparative Political Development

The Precedent of the West

G. LOWELL FIELD

Cornell University Press

Ithaca, New York

CORNELL UNIVERSITY PRESS

First published 1967

Library of Congress Catalog Card Number: 67–14082

PRINTED IN THE UNITED STATES OF AMERICA
BY W. F. HUMPHREY PRESS, INC.
BOUND BY VAIL-BALLOU PRESS, INC.

To My Wife

Preface

THE STUDIES leading to this book were provoked, at the time the author wrote a general text on governments, by a concern over the paucity of causal relations that could be stated with confidence in the field of comparative government.[1] Why had fascistic regimes occurred where they did and not elsewhere? Was there a sound reason for supposing that countries liable to fascistic take-over have more complex societies than those vulnerable to communistic revolution? Was there truly any reason for stable democratic regimes to occur mainly in highly industrialized societies or was such occurrence accidental? Could land reform, and a consequently satisfied peasantry, stabilize and democratize an otherwise unstable and undemocratic regime? Could mere prosperity, or economic development, do this?

A belief that a direct attack on this problem might be profitable was inspired by a suspicion that the historical political record was rich enough to support significant generalizations of a causal nature if the right concepts could be defined for analyzing it. Even if answers to the questions were merely lurking only a bit below the surface of current knowledge of political systems and of the societies in which the systems occurred (as strongly appeared likely to the author), the standard concepts used to classify political regimes or the

[1]*Governments in Modern Society* (New York, 1951).

societies in which the regimes occurred, or both, must not be the right ones for a profitable consideration of such matters. If the record did not show a clear relationship between "democracy" and "advanced society," for instance, or between "dictatorship" and "simple society," then so much the worse for such concepts as concepts. Instead of concluding that political matters are not amenable to causal analysis (a conclusion which for a variety of reasons tempts many humanists), one would propose heuristically that the wrong concepts were in use and would try others.

Thus the work reflected in this book was basically conceptual experimentation rather than empirical research. The empirical record to be explained was readily accessible. The problem was to make sense of it. At first, a limited body of historical material, mainly from the political histories of the major powers, was gone over many times to see how it looked in the light of differently defined concepts. It was like trying a variety of color filters to find one through which a distinct cloud pattern would become visible. The key discovery came to view gradually, namely that most regimes belong to a perdurant variety, those on the "main-stem of development"; their inherent characteristic is lack of legitimacy and consequent instability of political institutions. Such regimes should be seen as continuously "main-stem" and not as more or less democratic or more or less dictatorial, as they happen momentarily to appear. Serious work began about 1952. Three years later what came to be recognized ultimately as main-stem regimes were showing up, on an off-again on-again basis, when they happened to manifest particular characteristics (like large, but minority, Communist blocs in their legislatures). After eight years, improved concepts made this kind of regime visible steadily enough in certain instances to lead to a suspicion that it was really continuous in certain countries. The concepts necessary to make the main-stem regimes continuously visible as such were in use by 1962. The basic theory was completed by the following year. There remained for consideration just how to state it and just how much to claim for it.

The research was distinctly part-time, interspersed, as happened to be feasible, among teaching and administrative responsibilities. The project, long rather barren in output, must have tried the patience of many people—no doubt of my family, possibly of my secretary, Miss Florence Selleck (who has typed large portions of several versions of the manuscript), perhaps of my colleagues, and certainly of some of my students who were involved in various aspects of the research.

G. L. F.

The University of Connecticut
October 8, 1966

Contents

Comparative Political Development

The Precedent of the West

CHAPTER I

A Classification of Regimes

THIS BOOK applies modern conceptions of theory-construction and of model-building to the problem of classifying and explaining political systems. Contrary to what appeared to be the case to the innovators of the study of comparative government a half century and more ago, what primarily now calls for explanation is not the intricacy in conventional terms of constitutional variation, but the problem of what permits sufficient stability of institutional forms so that constitutional lore may be plausibly elaborated at all. It is not different forms of system so much as stability and change in systems—what may be expected to last and what may be expected to develop into something else—that constitute the basis of useful knowledge of political systems today.

Thus, a modern view of politics must be developmental, but there is a momentary awkwardness in referring to the present subject as "political development." This rubric is currently applied to discussions of the prospects of various newly independent, mostly non-Western, peoples. However, European political development has already taken place and may therefore be analyzed. The development of the new polities does not afford much data for study. Given the dominance of the West in all pragmatic fields of culture, it may turn out that, in spite of differences of circumstance, the European experience essentially forecasts the range of political possibilities for the non-Western world.

THEORY AS AGAINST COUNSEL

Deliberately to apply modern conceptions of theory-construction and of model-building to the present subject matter is to risk misunderstanding. Writers on comparative government have almost always expressed their ideas in the prudent language of policy and of advocacy. In sophisticated theory-construction, a statement is framed to serve a heuristic purpose rather than to convey information prudently to persons who may be supposed to be about to act upon it (perhaps imprudently).[1]

As political science becomes more sophisticated, readers will have to learn to distinguish theory from counsel. The basic difference in the grammar of these two forms of discourse lies in the expression of qualifications. Counsel that did not warn of the pitfalls of simplistic conceptions would be blameworthy. A theoretical statement that is highly or indefinitely qualified, however, is useless. It neither forms a premise for further deductions nor offers itself for refutation by any conceivable evidence.

[1]Bertrand de Jouvenel, in "On the Nature of Political Science," *American Political Science Review,* LV (1961), 773–779, and in *The Pure Theory of Politics* (New Haven, 1963), points out that theory-construction of the kind associated with the building of explicative models has been deliberately avoided by political philosophers for fear of acquiring knowledge about the manipulation of men that could fall into the wrong hands. After the era of Hitler and Stalin, however, he notes that politicians already know so much that anti-heuristic reticence should be abandoned.

Thus, in a theoretical context, a statement like the following will later be made: "A representative-consensual regime is stable." The theory within which such a statement occurs is offered for empirical validation only on the basis of a body of limiting assumptions, not all of which could practically have been fully foreseen and enumerated. If one should, therefore, observe a case in which a representative-consensual regime did in fact change into something else, the first question would be whether or not circumstances accompanying the event were excluded by the limiting assumptions or were such as might properly have been so excluded if they had been thought of. Only if the contrary event clearly occurred within the intended universe of discourse of the theory would it constitute an invalidation and require some modification in the theory.

An analogy in a field where theoretical sophistication has long been established is the law of falling bodies, according to which all bodies regardless of their different weights fall with equal velocities and with uniform acceleration. Yet, a feather does, in fact, fall more slowly in air than a piece of lead. The model, however, assumes a vacuum. Similarly, theoretical statements offered in this book as to the stability of a particular kind of regime assume that the regime exists in some polity reasonably like a modern nation-state. Thus, the 1966 collapse in Nigeria of a regime that might possibly have been classified, under the categories used in this book, as a representative-consensual regime need not, in view of the serious ethnic divisions in that country and the lack in most of its population of a sense of common nationality, be further analyzed to see whether it constitutes an invalidation of the theoretical statement that such regimes are stable.

UNIVERSE OF DISCOURSE OF THE THEORY

As a practical matter, the theory presented in this book is constructed to explain the political history of Western nation-states from about 1600 to the present. How much more widely this theory applies is left an open question. The limitation to nation-states is helpful because it allows one to set up rather simple theoretical constructs representing elite and mass in a political regime. Otherwise, the model would somehow have to represent the varying possibilities as to whether and to what degree there was in fact *one* elite, *one* mass, and *one* political system, and what trends might be going on toward further integration or disintegration on an ethnic or territorial basis with respect to elite, mass, and system separately or together.

No rigorous specification of the reference of "nation" or "nation-state" for present purposes seems necessary or possible. These value-laden terms are more commonly used in the manipulation than in the understanding of behavior. They are mostly in the possession of men of action. All that needs to be noted is that the various developments involved in the growth of national consciousness have given modern Western nation-states an organic unity that many earlier forms of state and many recently liberated countries lack.[2]

[2]The concepts of nation, national consciousness, nationalism, and nation-state owe much of their scholarly development to Hans Kohn, *The Age of Nationalism* (New York, 1962) and *The Idea of Nationalism* (New York, 1944, 1961); and Carleton J. H. Hayes, *Essays on Nationalism* (New York, 1926, 1933), *France: A Nation of Patriots* (New York, 1930), *The Historical Evolution of Modern Nationalism* (New York, 1931), and *Nationalism, a Religion* (New York, 1960). A useful description of historical developments relevant to these concepts as organizing rubrics is found in Friedrich Otto Hertz, *Nationality in History and Politics* (New York, 1944). Rupert Emerson has written an introduction to the problem of how these essentially Western concepts are likely to

People in a modern Western nation-state—whether elite or mass—see themselves as belonging for the most part to one common "nationality." A statement of strictly similar meaning would not be true for most ancient empires, for most medieval feudal kingdoms, and for many territories recently under colonial rule. This sensed ethnic unity of the population of a state presumably reflects some objective unity of culture and in most cases a common language, but it cannot be shown to be caused by some one or two readily identifiable objective factors. The theory in this book has neither been modified nor complicated to make it more applicable to polities less unified than those typical in the modern West.

The qualification as to nation-states may also serve to warn that the theory and model are not constructed with a view to explaining historical states of very small population or extent or purely tribal societies. It will be necessary for the model to refer to such polities both to firm up concepts by way of contrast and also as points of origin in possible chains of development, but the theory will have little to say about such entities that could be profitably tested against detailed factual evidence. Just as the present theory and model might (with greater or lesser modification) be found to be applicable to some ancient empire like that of the Assyrians, so someone might find it helpful with respect to the Athenian city-state or one of the Algonquin tribes. However, it is not claimed on the basis of the research so far conducted by the author that such applications would be altogether successful.

Examples in the present exposition will in general be confined to the political history of European nations from

---

prove useful in the analysis of the situations of the newly independent countries of Asia and Africa: *From Empire to Nation* (Cambridge, Mass., 1960).

about 1600 at the earliest or such later date as seems to mark in any particular case the emergence of a fully consolidated state that can be regarded as a nation-state. States of basically European cultural antecedents in parts of the world outside Europe will, however, be included: the United States, Canada, Australia, New Zealand, and (at least as they exist in the present century) the states of Latin America. Modern Japan will also be included since one may argue that it has rather completely assimilated the essentials of Western national organization along with Western technology and science.

States like Belgium, Canada, Russia, or Switzerland, which contain more than one linguistic community, will not be ignored on that account. However, if a discrepancy arose between their behavior and what the theory calls for and it could reasonably be explained by lack of cultural unity, these states could be treated as outside the universe of discourse. If the antagonism between Flemings and Walloons in Belgium continues to increase, it may produce events of a kind which the theory, as applied to Belgium, would not allow. Up to now, however, the theory seems to have held for Belgium (136 years since 1830) and for Switzerland (118 years since 1848) as well as for such linguistically unified states as France and the Netherlands. The theory thus seems likely to apply to a culturally composite state if something that passes for the subjective aspect of common nationality is present in sufficient degree. Nevertheless, no claim is made that the theory can be relied upon in such cases.[3]

[3]Clifford Geertz, in "The Integrative Revolution: Primordial Sentiments and Civil Politics in the New States," in Clifford Geertz, ed., *Old Societies and New States: The Quest for Modernity in Asia and Africa* (New York, 1963), pp. 105–157, complains that Rupert Emerson, *op. cit.*, pp. 95–96, defines a nation as a "terminal community—the largest community that, when the chips are down, effectively commands men's

The theory has not been constructed with a view to explaining the politics of polities that are not independent, whether these be detached areas governed under the authority of some distant state or local subdivisions of areas under more general governments. The ideas of the model may possibly prove applicable to cases of the latter kind, but this is speculative. The model does refer to dependent polities of firmly centralized administration, like those in recent European colonial empires, in much the same way that it refers to tiny states or tribal entities, that is, to something peripheral to its main reference, but the theory has little of an empirically verifiable character to say about them. In the historical examples systematically set forth, only polities that may be regarded as *de facto* independent are included.

No attempt will be made to demonstrate that the theory to be advanced is applicable without modification to the newly emerging independent states of Asia and Africa. It is possible that some aspects of the cultural traditions of the West determine the political behavior the theory purports to explain. On the other hand, this may eventually prove not to be true. The theory may in time prove to be reliably applicable to such of the new non-Western states as are consolidated in the future as fairly typical nation-states. At present, however, some pitfalls will be encountered in attempting to apply the theory to the non-Western states. In Chapter V these problems are discussed.

---

loyalties," claiming that this procedure merely shifts the ambiguity from "nation" to "loyalty" and leaves to the "determination of some future, unspecified historical crisis" the question of whether a particular state is a nation. This is, of course, what we do with respect to linguistically and culturally divided states. It seems all one could expect to do. Until something like full cultural uniformity has come about within the boundaries of a state, there can hardly be any assurance that future events will not pry it apart rather than cement it together.

The type of entity represented in the model and referred to by the theory is called by the newly revived term, "polity." The term, "community," although sometimes used in the simple sense of a politically organized territory (as by Robert M. MacIver) has recently been pre-empted by those associated with Karl W. Deutsch in the effort to analyze what produces the kind of unity exemplified in modern nation-states.[4] In their usage a "community" of various degrees of effectiveness may embrace more or less territory than is administered by one government. The term, "state," is also unavailable for present purposes because of its well established legal meaning. The Norwegian polity was independent *de facto* for internal purposes (under the operational criteria to be later advanced) from the 1880's, as was Canada perhaps from the 1860's, but in legal terms they were not ordinarily regarded as states until much later. Moreover, the British state has legally included many dependencies that would be no part of the polity—the home area and population of the United Kingdom—to which the theory and model might refer.

A polity for present purposes is a population (elite and mass) in a geographically distinct territory, embraced in a single distinct set of governing institutions. In any geographic context only the largest and most inclusive entity, if really possessed of *governing* institutions, is intended. Thus, a polity cannot be included in another polity, though its gov-

[4]Robert M. MacIver, *The Modern State* (Oxford, 1926), *Community* (New York, 1931), and *The Web of Government* (New York, 1947); Karl W. Deutsch, *Nationalism and Social Communication* (New York, 1953), *Political Community at the International Level* (Garden City, N. Y., 1954), and *Political Community and the North Atlantic Area* (Princeton, 1957); Karl W. Deutsch and William J. Foltz, eds., *Nation-Building* (New York, 1963).

erning institutions could bear some relation of subordination to those of another geographically distinct polity. In the extreme case of a fully dependent polity, however, as has been indicated, the theory has little of interest to say. Thus, the theory may be applied to a simple unitary state like Spain under normal circumstances but not to such a country as a mere geographic entity, for instance, during a period of civil war. At such a time, the theory might apply separately to each belligerent regime if it had enough stable organization to qualify under the definition of a polity. The theory applies to a federation, like the United States today or Australia, in which the central institutions are in practice dominant. It would not be likely to be relevant to some looser union of states like the United Nations or the United States before the Constitution took effect, nor to various historical complexes of feudal fiefs. It might very likely prove applicable to some of the more simple ultimate territorial entities in such a complex. Similarly, the theory presumably has no relevance to strictly international events.

WHY THEORIZE FORMALLY?

If such care as the previous pages manifest is required to specify a universe of discourse, what is the utility of introducing formal theorizing and model-building into such a subject matter as comparative government? Before any findings such procedures may uncover can prudently be made the basis for action, it would be well, in any case, for the whole situation to be evaluated in the terms already familiar to the historian, the political commentator, and the statesman. Why not, then, as has been customary in historical and political matters, retain the same intellectual procedures for seeking new knowledge as for its application?[5]

There would be no reason to substitute the language of theory for the language of counsel and evaluation if theory were only to serve a descriptive purpose, that is, if true theorizing consisted merely in describing the familiar in unfamiliar terms. The utility of formal theorizing and model-building, however, is to "postulate" rather than to "describe," and it has been the successful (if originally unintended) exploitation of this possibility in theoretical thinking, rather than mere accuracy in description, which made possible the great intellectual advances of the natural sciences.

Some matters of fact, including the concrete aspects of every concrete situation, may be directly observed. They need only be described in order to be recorded or transmitted. Statements about them are, in principle, directly subject to confirmation or refutation by further direct observation. As long as one stays with this sort of thing, one is not theorizing in

[5]Alexander H. Leighton, *Human Relations in a Changing World* (New York, 1949), pp. 152–155, points out that the thinking of policy-makers as compared with that of scientists is more rationalistic and less empiricist. We would say that the policy-maker at the moment of decision can only be a rationalist. When an accepted theory is about to be applied in making a policy choice, the time has gone by when it might have been tested empirically. The only sense in which policy-making can be made scientific lies in the activity of investigators before the time of a given policy choice in establishing reliable theories which administrators will know, believe in, and apply. The advancement of knowledge and its application are thus processes different in kind, the one empiricist, the other rationalist. Our viewpoint, therefore, does not admit the strict propriety of the term "policy sciences" used to characterize an approach initiated by Harold D. Lasswell, which approach nontheless has many affinities with that in the present book. See especially, Daniel Lerner *et al., The Policy Sciences* (Stanford, 1951); Harold D. Lasswell and Abraham Kaplan, *Power and Society* (New Haven, 1950); and Lasswell, *The Future of Political Science* (New York, 1963).

any serious sense whether one talks in common language or in an esoteric terminology. There are, however, as the revelations of modern science have made clear, facts of another order, namely, rather complex operational relationships which as wholes are not really observable at all and which can only be validated or refuted indirectly by first imagining the relationships ("postulating" them), then deciding what their observable consequences would be, and finally looking in appropriate situations to see whether these deduced consequences, in fact, occur. The social sciences have hardly begun to exploit this intellectual method of proceeding.

In the preceding exposition, the facts of national consolidation—the degree to which a polity approximates a typical modern nation-state—have been treated as matters of direct observation. It has been assumed that they can be taken into account in appropriate cases without any unusual intellectual procedures. Another range on a scale of unity and disunity, however, will appear later as a postulation of the theory. This is a difference in the way in which political elites in different polities take an ideological or nonideological view of their own relations with each other. It is not (in any accurate sense) a directly observable matter if only because of the discretion with which responsible persons normally conceal their own intimate motivations (perhaps even from themselves). To present this feature of elite motivation as a possible explanation of conduct is to postulate it. If such a postulation is to be validated or invalidated empirically, this cannot occur by direct observation. Rather, the consequences of the postulation must be elaborated by logical reasoning so as to bring out what consequences would be observable. If the postulated behavior, while not strictly confirmable in and of itself, serves indirectly to explain much that is directly observable and is not otherwise explicable (or as cogently explicable), then the postulation itself indirectly acquires credibility. This is the only sense in which the elaborate theories of modern physical science can be said to have been confirmed empirically.

FORM OF THE THEORY

In general form, the theory to be presented treats political regimes as belonging to three types: consensual, main-stem, utopian. It treats the socioeconomic levels of the polities in which the regimes occur as measurable according to a scale involving four distinct levels. In practice, however, there are intermediate stages between each pair of levels. Thus, if the intermediate stages are counted, there are seven levels. A polity acquires one of the three general types of regime in some relatively extraordinary event, usually the attainment of independence. Except through the massive intrusion of force supported from outside the polity, as in international or fully organized civil warfare, a polity before reaching Level 4 almost never shifts from one of these types of regime to another.

The levels modify the general types of regime. Level 1 produces a nonbureaucratic variant of the consensual type, the citizen-community, and of the main-stem type, the traditional regime. There is also a weakly bureaucratized variant of the utopian type, the radical-egalitarian regime, but this is a temporary aberration from a main-stem polity at Level 2 produced by what may be regarded as a politically induced temporary reversion to Level 1. Such a polity shortly reverts to Level 2, either resuming a main-stem type of regime or retaining the utopian type.

Regimes of consensual type have not been found to be distinctly modified by differences of level above Level 1. The consensual variant above Level 1 is called the representative-consensual regime. There is also only one utopian variant occurring above Level 1, the totalitarian regime.

Level 2 determines a special form of the main-stem type of regime called the dichotomized regime. Above this level, two main-stem variants occur, one called a trichotomized regime with a right, the other a trichotomized regime without a right.

Regimes of three of the main-stem variants, the traditional regime, the dichotomized regime, and the trichotomized regime with a right, are liable to upset by military coups and very simple rebellions. However, after such an event the succeeding regime is almost invariably of the same type as its predecessor. A representative-consensual regime, a totalitarian regime, and a trichotomized regime without a right, in contrast, are immune to simple types of irregular seizure of power.

Description of historical events does not yet fully confirm Level 4 as a distinct level. It is postulated because the reasoning of the model, which explains the other features of the occurrence of the types of regimes, suggests rather strongly that only representative-consensual regimes are viable at that level. There is as yet no clear case of a polity with one of the other general types of regime approaching Level 4 and then acquiring a representative-consensual regime without the interruption of the polity by some extraordinary event like temporary occupation by foreign forces.

As will be gathered from Diagram 1, which shows the terms of the theory relating to observables, the theory rests little on familiar concepts. Its exposition, therefore, presents a fairly wide choice in respect to the order of presentation of materials. It has seemed best to begin with the observables first, that is, to define the relevant terms and then to apply them to the description of actual polities in respect to regimes and levels. In this way, the bringing out of regularities in the developmental process, which previous terminology does not reveal, will show the need for a new theory before any attempt is made to present the theory proper in the sense of a set of explicative assumptions.

Diagram 1. Summary of the terms of the theory referring to observables

Type of regime	Socioeconomic level*		
	Level 1	Level 2	Level 3 or Level 4
Consensual	Citizen-Community	Representative-Consensual	
Main-Stem	Traditional	Dichotomized	Trichotomized without a right
			Trichotomized with a right
Utopian	Radical-Egalitarian	Totalitarian	

*The eight detailed types of regimes are shown at the levels in which they should occur under the theory except that Level 4 is not shown separately from Level 3.

In the remainder of this chapter, operational rules for classifying actual regimes among the eight types are presented. In Chapter II the concepts of working-force structure on the basis of which the levels are postulated and by means of which they are identified are set forth. Chapter III applies these concepts to show the historical course of development of European nation-states and nation-states of European antecedents. This factual exposition will show what the theory is called upon to explain. In Chapter IV the theory is presented, and its possible implications for the newly independent and the largely undeveloped countries are discussed in Chapter V. The final chapter deals with implications of the theory for the most highly developed countries.

TYPES OF REGIMES

For the classification of regimes, as in any other kind of phenomena, a practically infinite number of schemes could be devised. Every classification rests upon the selection of certain abstract features to serve as criteria. The utility of a classification, however, arises from its explicative force when associated with an appropriate theory. The classification of regimes into the three types here presented arose out of a process of conceptual experimentation whose aim was to find a classification that lent itself to the explanation of political stability and change and that showed a relation between types of regimes and levels of socioeconomic development in the countries where they occurred. This classification largely ignores constitutional structure and it does not seek to distinguish regimes accurately on the basis of how democratic they might be judged to be. Its criteria relate rather to the stereotypes through which political activity is perceived by participants. It rests in part upon a judgment that such viewpoints and their consequences in action represent major stabilities of politics. It has been adopted, however, because it serves the purpose of explanation in connection with a theory that can be validated by evidence. While the more familiar classifications seem more directly relevant to normative choices, they do not lend themselves to the generalized explanation of what actually occurs and the range of possibilities limiting political events.[6]

[6]Heuristically, the basic procedure used in constructing the theory may be called "experimental naming." Both the types of regimes and

Regimes will be classified into three main categories. One will be called "consensual" because, although different political positions may be taken in public discussion by influential persons, the operation of a regime of this type gives the strong impression that the influential are unified by a consensus as to ultimate political values.[7] A second category may be called "main-stem" because its variants form a line of development through which the older nation-states have passed. The style of political contest in regimes of the main-stem type suggests a dissension among the influential on ultimate values. A basis

---

the levels of socioeconomic development—the dependent and independent variables of the theory—were arrived at by specifying, testing, and revising concepts over a period of ten years. Successive bodies of students applied successive sets of concepts revised from year to year to a wide range of political data. Concepts were tested in this way for lack of ambiguity and for explicative relevance. This procedure was suggested by John Dewey and Arthur F. Bentley, *Knowing and the Known* (Boston, 1949), an epistemology in which knowledge is largely equated with successful naming.

[7]It is irrelevant to our argument whether consensus can be demonstrated to exist in any political system without circular reasoning. We are inclined to agree with Carl J. Friedrich, *The New Belief in the Common Man* (Boston, 1942), that it cannot. That consensus *appears* to exist in some systems constitutes the kind of social datum which we have called a "fact-fiction" or "organizing concept of social life" in "Law as an Objective Political Concept," *American Political Science Review*, XLIII (1949), 229–249. This is a kind of fact peculiar to the social sciences, a conventional idea whose referent is obscure or lacking but which is factual by virtue of its acceptance as a standard of reference in perception and in judgment. Such an idea serves to organize conscious purpose rather than to explain. *The fact that such an idea is held,* the sense of our textual definition of a consensual regime, however, may serve in explicative argument. For the most part, the data we specify as criteria for the recognition of all three types of regime relate to "organizing concepts" shaping the behavior of political participants. In applying the classification, it is essential that attention not be diverted from the way politics looks to participants by a search for factual referents for the stereotypes imputed to participants.

for serious civil conflict in discordant value systems appears to be present even when (apparently through a balance of forces) some degree of institutional stability prevails.[8] The third category of regimes may be called "utopian" because in regimes of this type all influential persons profess some one utopian position. While different practical positions may sometimes be expressed in such a regime, all argument refers to the standard of an ideal and imaginary goal which can be characterized only abstractly.[9] Such a regime gives no clear evidence of dissension within the influential, and it also fails to indicate plausibly that a real consensus exists, because any departure in public expression from the generally professed ideals would obviously be severely punished.

UTOPIAN REGIMES

A regime is classified as utopian if all influential persons profess a particular ideology although this ideology is known to be only one of several historical alternatives. The essential point is that profession of the historically specific ideological position is obviously compulsory in the sense of being required as a condition of playing any leadership role, however slight, or exercising any acquired influence over persons. In

[8]As with consensus in a consensual regime, so dissension in a mainstem regime is observable as a way in which things are seen by participants. Its factual reference in specifiable conflicting principles need not be demonstrable.

[9]To say that a regime has a utopian ideology is more nearly a judgment of the observer (rather than merely a judgment of how things look to participants) than is the case with a finding of consensus or dissension. However, in practice it will presumably be clear that participants also view their ideology in this light. In any case, in the operational rules for classifying regimes, it will not be necessary to use the term "utopian," since any ideology enforced against known alternative positions seems to meet the requirement of distinguishing these regimes.

the usual and often perdurant form, the totalitarian regime (e.g., Russia after the suppression of the Kronstadt mutiny in 1921), the ideological line is set specifically by the current utterances of those persons in highly authoritative positions. It is these utterances to which the aspirant influential person or the ambitious person must listen in order to conform his own statements, if possible, to what is required. In this form the ideology can vary widely in tone and content, as the contrast between German Nazism and Italian Fascism, on the one hand, and Soviet Communism, on the other, illustrates. The other variant of the utopian type of regime, the ephemeral radical-egalitarian regime (e.g., France from 1792 to 1794), involves a highly extreme egalitarianism of utterance on the part of all those forces that dare to assert themselves after a collapse of a former institutional pattern and social order. This is a vaguer but more rigid kind of ideology which no one is able to manipulate for current purposes with the same freedom as in a totalitarian regime, since at the moment no fully accepted authoritative positions or personal leaders exist.

MAIN-STEM REGIMES

The typical main-stem regimes, that is, those of all variant forms except the trichotomized regime without a right, are characterized by the existence of some more or less visible personalized center of power effectively commanding organized coercive forces and also by the fact that this center of power is willing and able to use such forces to make itself the ultimate arbiter of political decision-making regardless of institutional forms. The term "right" will be used to refer to this center of power and also to any wider political force or grouping clearly associated with and including it. The existence of a right *in this sense* in a main-stem regime is merely the other side of the coin from the strictly correlative fact that institutional arrangements for political representation and decision-making do not carry overwhelming legitimacy for all important parts of the elite as they do (except as ethnic or geographic divisions may be acute) in both utopian and consensual regimes. The simple mutiny of *intact* forces (that is, the mutiny of troops under their regular officers as distinguished from rank and file mutiny) or the simple mass uprising (rendered effective by the refusal of intact military forces to intervene) or at least the calculation that such events are practical possibilities are the distinctive marks of a typical main-stem regime.

The right, as just defined, in a typical main-stem regime takes one of two observable forms. Most commonly under recent social conditions it is simply the top level of the military-bureaucratic structure, capable of making a decisive display of force at will. Such a right has no necessary ideological color in the public clash of viewpoints and no necessary association with any popular political tendency. The top military commanders may, in fact, in such instances profess to be "liberal" (i.e., socially critical and usually anticlerical), as has frequently been the case with the most arbitrary dictatorships in Latin America. This kind of right will be called a "*de facto* right" since it comes about merely through the facts of pure power in a regime lacking institutional legitimacy. It may be called a "right" without implausibility because, like a traditionalistic ruling force, it seems regularly to veto what it regards as dangerous social experiments even though it may lack any clearly professed commitment to a socially conservative ideological position.

The other form of right, historically common but currently rare, centers around a traditional personal ruler who is normally associated with a hereditary, more or less leisured, aristocratic class. This type of right will be called a "traditionalist-personalist right." It is probably only a special case of the *de facto* right since violent usurpation is not an uncommon form of political action in monarchies, but often the appearanec of stability and of legitimate authority is so great in one of these cases that it would be misleading in observation to rely upon the similarity. (It was in relation to regimes of this kind that the idea of "legitimacy" was first seriously elaborated, probably because, in fact, legitimacy, in the sense of authority accepted without calculation, does not reliably inhere in personalistic rule.) The traditionalist-personalist right ordinarily has a clear association with a socially conservative ideological position and often represents the effective leadership of a substantial popular political tendency, especially if this association of popular following with aristocratic leadership is maintained through the apparent threat of other forces to popular religious practices and affiliations.

One or the other form of right, *de facto* or traditionalist-personalist, is the necessary and sufficient mark of a typical main-stem regime. It is necessary, however, to distinguish the contrived type of hereditary chief executive like the English king after 1689 or the Swedish king after 1809. In these cases, for the sophisticated elite participant in government at least, the authority of the monarch is derived from the general institutional structure and not *vice versa*. There is, therefore, in such a case neither a traditionalist-personalist right nor a *de facto* right, and the regime is, therefore, not a typical main-stem regime, that is, it is neither traditional, nor dichotomized, nor trichotomized with a right.

The three variant forms of the main-stem regime with a right are distinguished according to the stereotype under which the right is seen in relation to other political forces.

In the traditional regime, the lack of bureaucratic organization means that authority is for the most part amateur. The forces at the disposal of the right are essentially the weapons, skills, and leisure personally possessed by the dominant aristocracy. Commanding or prestigious functions are performed on a part-time basis by members of the aristocracy, who otherwise have little to do. Consequently, they often have no skills or interests in relation to the practical affairs of everyday life of the common people. Offices of more or less authority, locally at least, must therefore be filled in one way or another by common persons, that is, by peasants or artisans, in order that essential public services may be performed. These also are largely part-time positions, their incumbents providing their own support in the same kinds of work that involve their neighbors. There is thus an incipient dichotomy among the authorities of a traditional regime analogous to what becomes sharp in a dichotomized regime. Members of the aristocracy perform the functions and make the decisions that they think may be of importance to themselves. Members of the common people also exercise authority in matters that concern themselves but which are not of interest to the leisured class. Decisions of the first type of authority tend to preserve the allocation of privilege in society. Decisions of the second type tend to undermine it.

In a dichotomized regime (e.g., France in the early and middle nineteenth century) some degree of urbanization and enough productivity (or at least a sufficient local concentration of products) make it possible for some persons to spend their waking time in the exertion of authority. Since some do, all who would be effective must. All effective exercises of authority or of influence must be essentially full-time activities. The right-left stereotype now becomes a much more cogent and unavoidable stereotype than in a traditional regime. A "left," that is, a body of influential persons identified with a "rationalist-institutionalist" (as distinguished from a "traditionalist-personalist") attitude is now generally recognized as existing. It permeates (openly or covertly) all organizations. The more influential places open to it—bureaucratic and journalistic positions, teaching posts, as well as legal and medical professional practices—tend, in fact, to be occupied by members of relatively well-to-do urban families. In manners and morals, some of these families amount to a secondary aristocracy such as the original Whigs in seventeenth-century England. They are the "left" but they are in no sense weak or poor people. If the hereditary aristocracy survives, it remains distinct from the less ancient families leading the left. If it dies out or is forced from influence, as not uncommonly happens, its image continues. The rationalist-institutionalist left still sees itself as opposing the traditionalist-personalist right even after an objective observer can no longer identify the latter as a significant force. The *de facto* right (with or without serious justification) tends to be looked upon by the left as traditionalist-personalist.[10]

[10]What we generalize as characteristics of the main-stem regime and most typical in its dichotomized form have not infrequently been noted in more specific contexts in the past, particularly as characteristic of French as distinguished from British political attitudes. Thus, "The necessity for a radical break with the past in the pursuit of equality, instead of its gradual accommodation within continuing political institutions, left French society divided into mutually hostile segments, a situation that has ever since tended to make stable democratic government difficult" (Lloyd Fallers, "Equality, Modernity, and Democracy in the New States," in Geertz, ed., *Old Societies and New States,* p. 212). Here, as generally, the phenomenon is seen as more historically specific than we see it. In most states such divisive development has occurred. The attitude placing faction morally above polity, which the experience of such factionalization induces, then persists regardless of whether or not the objective division of factions on which it was based survives.

The belonging together of the "left," that is, of all socially critical and nontraditional forces, is the basic stereotype characterizing the dichotomized regime. The merchant of *laissez-faire* convictions and the doctrinaire Marxian Communist obviously "belong together" (however they may regard each other as misguided) because the serious opponent is viewed as the traditionalist-personalist right regardless of whether this continues as a serious political force or has been essentially replaced by a bureaucratic *de facto* right whose actual members may be publicly committed to liberalism. The concept "left" (not, of course, necessarily known by this name) embraces all socially critical and all actively humanitarian trends. In a dichotomized regime it is hardly thinkable that there could be other than two broad political tendencies: the left, broadly embracing all the rational and all the humane; and the strictly traditional right, viewed as a leisured and privileged class, whether the latter may actually exist as an assertive landed interest or may merely be believed to survive sheltered within the more secure niches afforded by either governmental bureaucracy (especially military careerism) or secure wealth.

When there continues to be a right (ordinarily *de facto* but rarely a traditionalist-personalist force associated with prestigious monarchical and bureaucratic institutions, as in the German and Japanese Empires) but when it is clear that the radically egalitarian left (usually socialist in doctrine and having a fairly clear-cut imagery of blue-collar supremacy) is a political tendency distinct from any merely rationalist-institutionalist trends of prosperous business or professional men, the regime is trichotomized with a right rather than dichotomized. There are now three political forces visible through customary stereotypes instead of only two. Besides the right *(de facto* or traditionalist-personalist) there is a distinct radical-egalitarian movement deriving its numerical support mainly from persons in manual employment in industry. In some cases, as in Japan between the World Wars, repression prevents this force from acquiring any secure organizational manifestation. The very measures used to repress it, however, fill in the stereotype and make clear the existence of a radical-egalitarian left as a potentially important political force. The third force in a trichotomized regime with a right will be referred to as a "center." It contains what remains of the former generalized leftism of the dichotomized regime—the rationalist-institutionalist tendencies now clearly differentiated from radically egalitarian trends. To varying degrees in different actual cases these rationalist-institutionalist tendencies are now mingled with and colored by attitudes (particularly on religious matters) that were associated with the traditionalist-personalist right. Such ideological mixture makes a clearly visible center like the Zentrum in Germany in the early part of this century, or the Mouvement républicain populaire (the M.R.P.) as well as Gaullism in France after World War II. Without this kind of mixture, the residual liberal left is difficult to distinguish from its generalized predecessor in a dichotomized regime (except by a more self-conscious commitment to the principle of property). Some countries have both kinds of a center: for example, the Catholic and Liberal parties of Belgium.

If there is neither a traditionalist-personalist right nor a *de facto* right (that is, if it is fairly clear that effective authority rests impersonally in more or less representative institutions) and if there does not exist the single imposed ideology of a utopian regime, then the regime can only be trichotomized without a right or consensual. The trichotomized regime without a right is recognized because the stereotypes of a trichotomized regime (viewing right, egalitarian left, and center as distinct forces) continue even though objectively there seems to be no right in the sense here used and, as a result, there occur rather commonly much sharper and more emotionally felt clashes between factions over policy than are usual in a consensual regime. As in Belgium throughout its history as an independent country, a trichotomized regime without a right possesses institutional stability in a form that is acceptable emotionally to no important faction or tendency. Ironically, those who cared little for democracy in principle have found that they can reliably count on winning elections. Hence, they have the authority to do effectively what a "right" seeks awkwardly to accomplish, that is, to ward off dangerous social experiments. Just as those who cared little for democracy now find it serving their purposes, those egalitarians who counted upon it ultimately to bring victory to their cause face the frustration of being a permanent minority. Thus, *de facto* stability of institutions is accompanied by a habit of periodical hopeless, ill-tempered demonstrations normally ending in riots. While conservative forces need not, and the egalitarians cannot, seriously challenge the authority of institutions, neither side accepts the morality of its opponents, and policy issues provoke highly divisive sentiments.

CONSENSUAL REGIMES

If there is not an imposed ideology, if there is no "right" in the special sense here used, and if the acerbities of factional bitterness carried over from a history of main-stem conditions do not prevail, the regime is consensual. Such a regime could be an unbureaucratized "citizen-community," the kind of regime, probably (if durable) always small in area and population, in which the whole citizen-body (by no means necessarily the whole population) participates on a fairly equal basis in making serious decisions and in which force to carry them out comes also essentially from the whole citizen-body under arms. Such have been many nonliterate tribes, some of the rural cantons of medieval Switzerland, the seventeenth century colonies of Connecticut and Rhode Island, and even to the present day Andorra. Citizen-communities, however, hardly ever occur under current conditions.

In the bureaucratized variant of the consensual type, the representative-consensual regime (for instance, the United States), there is a well established institutional pattern of authority and a tradition of political contest in which even the remembrance of a right in the sense here used plays no part. Authority is firmly associated with institutions rather than with particular persons, and simple seizures of power by force are unknown and not seriously thought about.

CRITERIA FOR CLASSIFYING REGIMES

Characterizations have now been supplied for all the types of regimes to which the theory refers. Especially because these concepts are all new and unfamiliar, it is desirable to lay down more precise operational rules for their recognition empirically. The following set of criteria has been tested in a variety of contexts. It appears to be unambiguous in normal contexts when there is a fair amount of information available about the politics of a polity. These criteria will be regularly referred to hereafter in all assignments of actual regimes to one or another type under the theoretical system. The criteria not only distinguish the eight types of regimes in independent polities; they also include a test for determining whether a regime is to be deemed dependent or independent and another for distinguishing the more dictatorial from the more constitutional variants of certain regime-types. This latter criterion is useful mainly to facilitate the enumeration of the number of different regimes over a given period of time and will be used in the present exposition only in the section of Chapter III where the relative instability of regimes of different types is considered.

CRITERION 1, *distinguishing Utopian regimes*

Only a single defined ideological position (of several known about in the polity) is allowed any public expression.

"Public" refers to more or less fluid elite circles as well as to contexts in which communication might reach the masses. "Defined" includes an extreme egalitarian sentiment widely asserted by a populistic revolutionary movement, but otherwise it means definitely prescribed, construed, and inculcated on the authority of a dominant organization or charismatic leader. An "ideological" position must be one designed more or less deliberately to have mass appeal, whether or not it may be judged socially conservative in intention. It does not include mere exegesis with respect to traditional cultural principles. It must have primary reference to the governmental regime and to governmental practices.

To say that only a single position is allowed expression means that rival authorities do not publicly take conflicting stands on current policy or political belief and that persons in authoritative, responsible, or influential positions seem habitually to look for cues as to the current line in the utterances of high officials and authorities and tend unhesitatingly to conform their own expressions of opinion to the positions indicated by such cues.

The tolerance of religious organizations whose activities are strictly limited and in which influential persons do not participate is compatible with this condition, as is the limited tolerance of literary and artistic expression that falls short of clearly stating rival political positions.

CRITERION 2, *distinguishing dependent regimes*

The executive is bureaucratically dependent upon that of another regime in such a way that force could readily be applied locally by a decision made outside the regime under consideration or the regime obviously accepts a practical subordination to outside power.

In the first case—bureaucratic dependency—local military and police forces are commanded by executive authorities actually dependent upon outside authority, as in the case of a typical colonial dependency. Note that this condition may be informally terminated by the establishment of full cabinet responsibility to a local legislature. It is irrelevant whether or not a regime conducts its own foreign relations or is internationally recognized as independent.

The second case—virtual subordination to outside power—includes regimes whose leading personnel see their powers as obviously existing at the sufferance of an outside power that could readily intervene by force and that clearly would be expected to do so if the policy of the local regime departed materially from its wishes. Commonly, the dominant power in such a case has occupying forces in the territory of the regime dominated, but this need not be the case if such forces could readily enter from nearby territories.

CRITERION 3, *distinguishing the nonbureaucratized regimes (i.e., the traditional, the citizen-community, and the radical-egalitarian)*

Criterion 2 does not apply and for much of the population much of the time, effective coercion is locally based and amateur rather than bureaucratically organized.

In the normal case this means that coercive power is essentially in the hands of leisured aristocrats or local notables or (in the case of very small populations) it can be exerted only by citizens assembled for the occasion. In other words, bureaucratically organized police and military forces are not important means of governance.

There is a special "revolutionary" case to which this criterion is applicable when a recent popular upheaval has very largely undermined the status order. In this case some bureaucratic and full-time military formations may persist, but their structure and discipline has been so undermined that they are likely to act spontaneously on political slogans, as do informal mobs, rather than in response to authoritative commands. Ordinarily in such a case, Criterion 1 will have been found applicable because of the assertion of extreme egalitarian sentiment, but this might not be true if the previous regime itself professed such an ideology. This special case terminates as soon as it is clear that disciplined coercive forces are reliably at the disposal of the central authorities.

In applying this criterion to normal nonrevolutionary cases, three possible situations may be distinguished. (1) The criterion is clearly applicable if the power structure is either one approximating direct democracy or one based in more or less feudal fashion upon interconnections among leading families. (2) The criterion is inapplicable if authority rests clearly in either a complex representative structure or in persons commanding bureaucratic military structures or in some combination of these forms. (3) In borderline cases, which consist of fairly large countries where there are central authorities of the second type but fairly large areas normally dominated by local authorities of the first type, the criterion is to be deemed inapplicable if and only if political factionalism and ideological appeals associated with personalities in the central government seriously involve masses of people beyond the central cities.

CRITERION 4, *alternative with Criterion 5 in distinguishing a main-stem regime with a right (i.e., one of the following: a traditional, dichotomized, or trichotomized with a right regime)*

Criterion 1 is not applicable and the major locus of discretionary political power is a monarchical court of traditional character.

For this criterion to be applicable, the ruler must essentially claim his powers as a personal possession on a traditional basis or by pure and simple right of conquest. A theocratic monarchy to whose ruler is imputed special personal authority is included. Otherwise, some sort of hereditary claim or aspiration on the part of the ruler is assumed, although there need not be automatic succession in a fixed line precluding any form of election among claimants. If, however, the ruling house is clearly known to be dependent historically upon choices made by other domestic institutional centers of power —whether representative structures or permanent military-bureaucratic structures—and merely forms one organ of an institutional power structure, it is not "traditional" in the sense intended and the criterion does not apply. The criterion may, however, apply regardless of personal usurpation and of the existence of pretenders apparently more legitimate than the incumbent ruler.

CRITERION 5, *alternative with Criterion 4 in distinguishing a main-stem regime with a right (i.e., one of the following: a traditional, dichotomized, or trichotomized with a right regime)*

Criteria 1, 2, and 4 are not applicable. Simple seizures of

power by persons commanding military forces are regarded as practical political possibilities.

This means that a reasonably well-informed participant would regard such events as within the range of practical politics. The applicability of Criterion 5 does not depend upon a prophecy that a *coup d'état* will actually occur within any finite time-period or at all, though the recent occurrence of coups will, of course, tend to make this criterion applicable unless suitable changes have subsequently occurred in the polity. In general, Criterion 5 tends to mean merely that organized military forces under bureaucratic command are in existence and that the institutionalized forms of authority in the current regime evidently carry no overwhelming legitimacy for the persons commanding such forces.

This criterion will be assumed to be true except in rather small countries clearly organized under tribal or fairly direct democratic institutions if Criterion 3 (nonrevolutionary case only) applies and Criterion 4 does not.

If an actual regime has been considered under the several criteria up to this point and the applicability or nonapplicability of each is determined, then the regime may be identified if it is totalitarian or one of the three nonbureaucratic types. Otherwise, the classification will have been determined up to a choice among not more than two regime-types. According to the criteria found applicable—among these five only—the regime-type or possible regime-types are indicated as follows:

Criteria applicable	*Type of regime*
1 only	Totalitarian
1 and 2	Dependent totalitarian
1 and 3	Radical-egalitarian

2 only (or 2 and 4)	Either dependent dichotomized or dependent trichotomized
3 only	Citizen-community
3 and either 4 or 5	Traditional
4 or 5 only	Either dichotomized or trichotomized with a right
none	Either trichotomized without a right or representative-consensual

Thus, two additional criteria are necessary: one to distinguish a dichotomized regime from a trichotomized regime with a right, and one to distinguish a trichotomized regime without a right from a representative-consensual regime. The latter will be presented first.

CRITERION 6, *distinguishing the trichotomized regime without a right*

None of the first five criteria are applicable and serious popular disorders—demonstrations, riots, etc.—provoked by governmental policy-decisions are regarded as practical political possibilities. The possibility of disorders resting solely on regional or ethnic divisions is to be ignored.

This criterion is to be understood in the same general sense as was indicated in the qualifications for Criterion 5. It does not depend upon a prophecy that major disorders will actually occur, but if such disorders have recently occurred, Criterion 6 is likely to apply unless suitable changes have subsequently occurred in the polity. In general, Criterion 6 tends to mean merely that the institutionalized forms of authority in the current regime carry no overwhelming legitimacy for persons who exercise effective leadership over important political forces.

Since this criterion can apply only to regimes to which none of the earlier criteria applied, it serves to distinguish those regimes to which it is applicable as trichotomized with a right and to indicate that other regimes to which none of the previous criteria applied are representative-consensual.

CRITERION 7, *distinguishing the dichotomized regime*

Neither of Criteria 1 and 3 applies but either Criterion 2 or one of Criteria 4 and 5 does. All positions taken on political questions tend to be regarded as falling into one of two distinct categories: the general viewpoint of a rationalist-institutionalist "left" and the general viewpoint of a traditionalist-personalist "right."

In practice this usually means that many influential persons in such moderately or highly prestigious or prosperous categories as doctors, lawyers, and businessmen, as well as most journalists, teachers, and secular intellectuals seem to adhere to an ideological viewpoint ("leftist" in the above sense) highly critical of important traditional statuses and institutions (e.g., aristocratic families, monarchy, church, etc.) and that this generalized and influential, socially critical, political tendency is not seen as clearly separated from such radical-egalitarian views as have, or appear to have, potential appeal to the low-status population. This is normally the observable form of the "left" in a dichotomized regime. The "right" in such a regime, as defined above as "traditionalist-personalist," may or may not be objectively identifiable.

However, the "left" may also not be clearly observable, at least from a great distance from the actual polity and through standard reference sources. It is likely, in fact, that circumstances refuting the applicability of this criterion, if they exist, will become noticed by the distant observer more than will positive evidence of its applicability in the case of many polities. Criterion 7, therefore, if its formal stipulations as to the applicability of other criteria are satisfied, is deemed applicable unless it is judged that a reasonably well-informed participant would find it necessary to recognize distinct and important political forces besides the generalized "left" and the "right" in the form of either a radical-egalitarian left, seen as quite distinct from the generalized but not radical-egalitarian antitraditional left, or important forces (usually with religious identification), a "center," that clearly mingle traditional with more or less socially critical appeals.

In the case of regimes determined under previous criteria to be either dichotomized or trichotomized with a right or either dependent dichotomized or dependent trichotomized, the applicability of Criterion 7 indicates the dichotomized condition and its nonapplicability, the trichotomized. The attentive reader will correctly infer that the original experimental form of Criterion 7 was written on the assumption that a dichotomized regime is more readily "observable," than is a trichotomized regime, at least in the materials in a general reference library. This is perhaps true for classic cases like France or Spain in the nineteenth century or Colombia more recently, where the "right" retains objective importance as a political force or movement. Commonly, however, this is not the case, and experience shows that it is best to presume a main-stem regime with a right to which Criterion 3 does not apply to be dichotomized unless positive evidence indicates that it is trichotomized.

Thus, Criteria 1 through 7 suffice to distinguish the eight detailed regime-types in independent polities and the three regime-types in dependent polities to which the theory refers.[11] For certain purposes, especially in relation to regimes like some of those in Latin America where frequent changes occur as between more or less representative and openly dictatorial forms, an additional distinction is useful. The applicability of the following criterion will indicate an "autocratic" form of regime in which the executive cannot be considered as constitutionally chosen or responsible. Since it does not relate to distinctions among the eight regime-types, this criterion will be arbitrarily numbered "20." The distinction it draws could not be made practically for a totalitarian regime and would serve no useful purpose with respect to the regimes to which Criterion 3 applies. Hence the distinction will be made only for the four nontotalitarian bureaucratized regimes.

CRITERION 20, *distinguishing "autocratic" forms of certain regime-types*

Neither Criterion 1 nor Criterion 3 applies, and a prudent and informed participant would regard the real executive authority as institutionally irremovable, that is, as removable only by *coup d'état* or revolution.

This is not intended to include chief executives serving for fixed terms merely for this reason. If, however, the office is for life or hereditary and involves substantial real executive power this criterion is applicable. In cases with traditional monarchies, Criterion 4 will already have been found applicable and in such cases Criterion 20 is necessarily applicable.

In cases where Criterion 5 has been found applicable and the administration in office dates from a coup and seems to

[11] It will be noted that as a matter of definition all nontotalitarian dependent regimes are assumed to be main-stem regimes with a right. It seemed a useless complication to allow a presumably empty category of "dependent consensual."

reflect the power of a military clique, Criterion 20 is applicable even if a subsequent formal election might be claimed to have legitimized the incumbent administration. In such a case, Criterion 20 remains applicable until the higher executive personnel seems to have been substantially changed as the result of popular election or parliamentary proceedings. The question in these instances is whether or not a military clique descended from that which seized power seems still to be substantially in control of the executive (but not merely in the sense that it would be able to carry out another coup to assert its power).

For Criterion 20 to be applicable, it is sufficient that the executive authority is institutionally irremovable within the territory of the polity. Thus, Criterion 20 applies in all cases of formally avowed dependency in which the chief executive authority is appointed by some outside power. In these cases Criterion 2 will have been found applicable.

It would probably be rare under present-day conditions to find Criterion 20 applicable in a case where none of Criteria 2, 4, or 5 applied. Such a case, however, could be a real but limited monarchy or a "dictatorship" in the original, purely temporary and constitutionally authorized sense of the term.

Criterion 20 will in general be ignored in the classification of actual regimes in the following exposition. It is introduced primarily so that it may be used in the section of Chapter III where consideration is given to the number of "different regimes" of a given regime-type that occur within a specified period of time, a measure of the institutional stability of the different regime-types.

CHAPTER II

Levels of Socioeconomic Development

THERE ARE many different ways in which the level of socioeconomic development of a country could be measured.[1] Often, economic development is discussed in terms of material products or of the monetary values involved in economic activities. It is people, however, who are governed politically. Thus, differences in the composition of populations seem likely to be more closely correlated with political behavior than differences in the amount and type of production. For some time it has been known that the composition of the working force undergoes definite changes as a country develops.[2] By a process of conceptual experimentation, ways were sought to classify the occupations and statuses

[1]For a statistical theory relating a number of available measures and a large tabulation of relevant data, see Karl W. Deutsch, "Social Mobilization and Political Development," *American Political Science Review,* LV (1961), 493–514. The use of research and development expenditure as an index of socioeconomic development is illustrated in Steven Dedijer, "Measuring the Growth of Science," *Science, CXXXVIII,* No. 3542 (1962), 781–787.

[2]See Colin Clark, *The Conditions of Economic Progress* (London, 1940), Chapter V, for historical studies of the shift of employment from primary and secondary to tertiary industries in the course of development.

making up a working force into categories whose variations could be used in the explanation of political stability and change. The classification that seems best to serve this purpose and which is presented in the present chapter involves the following categories and subcategories: (I) the autonomic component, comprising (A) an agricultural portion, and (B) a nonagricultural portion; and (II) the decision-audience, comprising (A) a manual portion, and (B) a nonmanual portion, made up of (1) a services portion, and (2) a white-collar portion.

The two subdivisions of the autonomic component and the two subdivisions of the nonmanual portion of the decision-audience must be taken into account in the practical handling of data, but they do not appear to have much explicative significance. The relative proportions of the two major categories—the autonomic component and the decision-audience—provide a continuous scalar measure of socio-economic level. We shall call this measure (expressed as the percentage of the decision-audience in a working force) "decision-audience value." Systematic variations, however, occur in the internal composition of the decision-audience as the latter increases. These produce distinct qualitative patterns of working-force composition in successive ranges of the scalar measure. As will be explained later, the relative proportions of three components—the autonomic component, the manual decision-audience, and the nonmanual decision-audience—allow the definition of four levels.

THE AUTONOMIC COMPONENT

Governance is an aspect of all human societies. The motivation of persons, and hence their conduct, is modified by the wishes, express or implied, of other persons. Governance is accomplished in part through internalized norms shared by participants in fairly intimate and homogeneous groupings. As internal controls, such norms either operate spontaneously or are activated by appropriate utterances of associates. Governance also operates through the more or less conscious response of persons to the express or implied wishes of other persons who could advantage or disadvantage them. This is governance by power. Governance by internalized norms and governance by power normally occur together, sometimes reinforcing and sometimes counteracting each other.

Within intimate and homogeneous groups, however, governance by power is seldom noticed, since its effect is normally to reinforce internalized norms. For persons whose daily lives are spent in familylike groupings, as in small farming and traditional artisanship, power comes to notice mainly as it impinges upon the intimate group from outside. In such cases, it does not normally reinforce internalized norms but usually appears as more or less arbitrary compulsion. Moreover, such exercises of power as affect such an intimate working group from the outside are in no way necessary to the regular work of the group. The work performed would go on (for the benefit of participants at least) even if there were no powerful persons in the social environment surrounding the group.

Even when a working organization is not a familylike structure, power is perceived in much the same way by persons whose regular work consists of discretionary manipulations of material objects or of portions of the natural environment. The skilled manual laborer working up resistant materials, the farm worker handling a plant or animal or patch of soil, the vehicle driver threading his way through traffic is necessarily following internalized norms and is primarily attentive to the material rather than to the social environment. While the general organization of his work may be determined by the wishes of an employer or supervisor, his detailed working operations are largely unsupervised. As with the worker in a familylike group, his attention is only sporadically directed to power. Exertions of power appear as intrusive upon his normal activities.

In every population the groupings just characterized—those who work in intimate groups and those who perform unsupervised operations on things rather than on persons—constitute a category of persons distinguished by an attitude toward power that is usually negative and uncomprehending. This category may be called the "autonomic component" because its members see themselves (as individuals or in small intimate groups) as capable of full autonomy in the decision of the ordinary matters of daily life. While they may yield to power, and even under some circumstances may approve of the effects of power, they do not see the relations produced by power as essential to normal living.

THE DECISION-AUDIENCE

Except in the simplest societies, however, the whole population does not belong to the autonomic component. There are always persons whose activities could not be meaningfully ordered at all except by the more or less conscious assessment of the probable motivations of socially remote persons. This residual category of persons may be called the "decision-audience" because, unlike the members of the autonomic component, its members are an attentive audience for the decisions, and for intimations of the probable decisions, of other persons. To the members of the decision-audience the power of persons over other persons is perceived, not as an extraneous intrusion upon normal activities, but rather as the matter-of-fact structure of everyday life.

Since power rests on power, is always to some extent balanced by power, and is seriously exercised only by the manipulation of the power of other persons, the really powerful are themselves always members of the decision-audience. So also are many types of service personnel whose activities are intimately associated with those of the powerful. Strictly professional occupations and white-collar employment necessarily belong to the decision-audience since work in these contexts is ineffective except as the motivations and behavior of other persons are successfully foreseen or manipulated. Beyond these categories, where members are directly involved in the meaningful exercise of power, in industrialized societies there is also a component of the decision-audience consisting of manual labor employed in routinized operations whose meaningful aspects are largely predetermined by supervision. Lacking individual discretion in the work processes in which they are occupied, the attention of persons engaged in routinized manual labor tends to center upon their social relations with each other and with employers and work supervisors.

COMPOSITION OF A WORKING FORCE

In principle, the members of a working force may be classified as follows:

1. Certain occupational groupings may be assumed to belong to the autonomic component. These include agriculture, really skilled manual labor, and a variety of minor categories such as vehicle drivers, custodians of buildings, guides, trappers, hunters, and other types whose detailed activities are oriented toward the material environment and are largely by their nature exempt from effective supervision.

2. Certain occupational groupings may be assumed to belong to the decision-audience. These include really learned

professional occupations in which practice depends largely upon verbal skills exercised in dealing with other persons and all types of bureaucratic personnel—managerial, administrative, and clerical—operating in the context of large-scale organization. Personnel exclusively engaged in salesmanship probably also belong necessarily to the decision-audience.

3. The residual occupational categories, such as manual labor that is not highly skilled and that is readily subject to supervision, a wide variety of service personnel, and entrepreneurs and their immediate associates in activities that are not primarily dependent upon verbal skills, can be classified as between the two basic categories only on the basis of the type of working group in which they participate. Those whose working environment is a small-scale, familylike grouping belong to the autonomic component. Those whose work is oriented to a large-scale and impersonal organizational complex belong to the decision-audience.

DECISION-AUDIENCE VALUE—PREFERRED FORMULA

As has been indicated, "decision-audience value" means a number that expresses the percentage of a working force belonging to the decision-audience. Naturally, an exact decision-audience value can be secured from available statistics only by a conventional rule. Data are never available with reference to all the subdivisions of a working force that might be relevant to determining a decision-audience value. Moreover, no conceivable enumeration could satisfy us completely that all persons in certain categories were members of the decision-audience while all others were autonomic. While this twofold division of the members of a working force appears to have basic significance in generalized explanation, one can hardly assume that every person, considered individually, clearly and obviously belongs to one category rather than to the other.

The preferred formula for computing decision-audience value was designed to apply to what appears to be the largest body of relevant comparable data. This consists of the various reports of working forces in different countries which are cross-classified as to occupation and socioeconomic status published in several annual numbers of the United Nations *Demographic Yearbook.*[3]

In defining the autonomic component and the decision-audience in earlier passages we made use of both the occupation a person performs and the type of working group in which he participates. In computing a decision-audience value it is neither practical nor necessary to take into account most of the occupational categories referred to. The occupations other than farming that belong to the autonomic component regardless of the nature of the working group—truly skilled manual labor and certain other cateories—are seldom distinguished in actual enumerations and are probably not very numerous in any working force nor very variable in proportion when different working forces are compared. The same considcrations apply to those occupational categories that necessarily belong to the decision-audience. Administrative and clerical personnel in large-scale organizations cannot be

[3]Statistical Office of the United Nations, New York, various dates; except first 1948 number (Lake Success, New York, 1949). Suitable data appear in Table 15 of the 1956 number and Table 13 of the 1964 number. Similar tabulations, in some cases using industrial rather than occupational categories, appear in Table 12, 1964 number; Table 16, 1955 number; Table 13, 1949–50 number; and Table 12, 1948 number. None of the unmentioned numbers (through the 1964 number) contain suitable data. The argument of this chapter was completed before the 1964 number was available.

distinguished in many enumerations from a numerous body of small entrepreneurs, many of whom presumably belong to the autonomic component. While the learned professions are more often distinguished in actual enumerations, they are a small percentage of the working force. Taking them into account in the general formula would suggest a descriptive accuracy exact decision-audience values do not possess.

Thus, the only occupational category important enough and variable enough to require consideration in determining decision-audience values is agriculture. In the preferred formula all persons engaged in agriculture as an occupation are treated as belonging to the autonomic component. This procedure is, of course, not strictly accurate. There is, however, no practical way of shaving off any portion of the agricultural occupational category that may properly belong to the decision-audience. The only practical alternative procedure would be to distribute agricultural personnel between the two categories in the same way nonagricultural personnel are distributed. This method of computing decision-audience values was tried experimentally before the present procedure was decided upon. The present procedure yields a set of values supporting a general explicative theory of political stability and change, and the relative values for different countries are generally consonant with what appear on other grounds to be their relative levels of socioeconomic advancement. A set of values computed without distinguishing agriculture from other occupations does not appear to support any explicative theory and contains implausibilities in the ranging of countries relatively to each other.

If the agricultural component of a working force is treated as belonging entirely to the autonomic component, the distribution of the rest of the working force between the two categories may be closely estimated by treating self-employed persons and unpaid family workers as a measure of the autonomic component outside agriculture. The great majority of such persons may be assumed to work in family-type enterprises. A descriptively more plausible value will, however, be secured if an allowance of one half the self-employed is added to take account arbitrarily of paid employees in midget enterprises (in effect, one such employee being allowed for each two such working groups). This overweighting of the self-employed also results in reducing somewhat the effect of reported unpaid family workers, a category whose reported size unquestionably varies seriously according to cultural stereotypes, in ranging different populations relatively to each other. With these deductions for the autonomic component, decision-audience value is the residual percentage.[4]

The preferred formula for computing a decision-audience value may thus be expressed as follows:

$$da = 100 - ag - ac$$
$$ac = 1\tfrac{1}{2}\, se + ufw,$$

where *da* stands for decision-audience value and the other symbols represent the following as proportions of the working force:

ag—persons in agricultural occupations, *ac*—the nonagricultural autonomic component, *se*—the self-employed outside agriculture, *ufw*—the unpaid family workers outside agriculture.

[4]To visualize more clearly the nature of these measures, note that the entire working force consists of paid workers, self-employed persons, and unpaid family workers. Then, the decision-audience is the paid workers outside agriculture reduced by one for every two midget enterprises outside agriculture, while the autonomic component consists of all persons working in agriculture plus the self-employed and unpaid family workers outside agriculture and one paid worker for every two midget enterprises outside agriculture.

DECISION-AUDIENCE VALUES COMPUTED BY THE PREFERRED FORMULA

Table 1 shows all decision-audience values that could be computed for independent countries by the preferred formula from data published in the several annual numbers of the United Nations *Demographic Yearbook* before the 1964 number appeared.[5] It also shows the percentage values for the agricultural component of the working force and for the autonomic component outside agriculture from which the decision-audience values were computed. Entries are ranged in order of decision-audience values from lowest to highest. Table 2 supplements the entries in Table 1 for populations in the same source that meet the requirements for Table 1 in all respects except that the agricultural classification in the data is industrial rather than occupational. Probably most of these decision-audience values are identical with or very slightly lower than those that would be secured from occupational data.[6]

THE ESTIMATION OF DECISION-AUDIENCE VALUES

Data such as were used in Tables 1 and 2 for the computation of decision-audience values under the preferred for-

[5]Only countries that were at least nominally independent within an eleven-year interval centered on the census date are included. Besides data for dependent countries, we passed over a number of tabulations that failed to make distinctions necessary for the formula, that contained a large proportion of unclassified persons, or that referred only to a defined portion of the total working force, such as the urban working force.

[6]For the eighteen sets of data presented in full industrially in Table 16, 1955 number, *Demographic Yearbook,* and occupationally in Table 15, 1956 number, computed *da* was identical in seven cases, lower by one when based on industrial data in seven cases, lower by two in one case, higher by one in two cases, higher by two in one case.

Table 1. Decision-audience values computed by the preferred formula from occupational data*

Country and date	Decision-audience value (*da*)	Autonomic component outside agriculture (*ac*)	Agricultural component (*ag*) (occupational)
Pakistan 1951	2	22	76
Thailand 1947	4	12	84
Haiti 1950	5	10	85
Honduras 1950	8	9	83
Bulgaria 1934†	9	11	80
Guatemala 1950	15	18	67
Paraguay 1950	20	25	55
Poland 1931†	21	14	65
El Salvador 1950	22	15	63
Finland 1940†	25	18	57
Ecuador 1950	32	18	50
Japan 1950	32	20	48
Panama 1950	32	14	54
Costa Rica 1950	33	13	54
Venezuela 1950	37	24	39
Hungary 1941†	38	14	48
Cuba 1953	40	19	41
Ireland 1936†	40	12	48
Chile 1952	45	26	29
Finland 1950	46	8	46
Israel 1948	51	37	12
Norway 1930†	51	14	35
Austria 1951	52	15	33
Denmark 1950	57	18	25
Sweden 1950	67	13	20
Canada 1951	68	13	19
Australia 1947	69	16	15
New Zealand (Euro.) 1945	69	11	20
United States 1950	74	14	12
United Kingdom 1951	86	8	6

*All data except as otherwise indicated are from Table 15, 1956 number, *Demographic Yearbook*. If data included unemployed persons, these were, if possible, excluded. Persons outside agriculture but unclassified as to status (paid, unpaid, self-employed) were excluded from the total in computing *ac* but included in computing *ag*.

†Data for these items come from Table 12, 1948 number, *ibid.* While the classification in these cases is occupational, managerial, administrative, clerical and sales personnel are not systematically segregated, as in the data from the 1956 number. The *ag* figures in these cases may therefore be slightly higher than would be strictly comparable with the other data.

Table 2. Decision-audience values computed by the preferred formula from industrial data*

Country and date	Decision-audience value (*da*)	Autonomic component outside agriculture (*ac*)	Agricultural component (*ag*) (industrial)
Colombia 1938 †	10	16	74
Yugoslavia 1931 †	12	9	79
Rumania 1930 †	14	7	79
Bolivia 1950 §	15	13	72
Peru 1940 †	15	23	62
Nicaragua 1950 §	18	14	68
Egypt 1947 §	19	21	60
Philippines 1948 §	21	8	71
Mexico 1950 §	24	18	58
Brazil 1950 §	25	14	61
Yugoslavia 1953 §	28	5	67
Japan 1947 §	30	17	53
Italy 1936 †	33	19	48
Portugal 1940 †	40	11	49
Portugal 1950 §	40	12	48
Ireland 1951 §	49	11	40
Czechoslovakia 1947 †	51	11	38
Argentina 1947 §	52	23	25
Denmark 1940 †	54	17	29
Luxemburg 1947 §	54	20	26
East Germany 1946 §	56	15	29
Liechtenstein 1950 §	56	22	22
Netherlands 1947 ‡	57	23	20
Norway 1946 §	57	14	29
Sweden 1940 †	57	14	29
New Zealand 1936 †	58	15	27
Germany 1939 †	59	15	26
Switzerland 1941 †	59	20	21
Australia 1933 †	60	19	21
Canada 1941 †	60	13	27
Norway 1950 §	60	14	26
Belgium 1947 §	61	27	12
West Germany 1950 §	61	16	23
Sweden 1945 ‡	64	12	24
Switzerland 1950 §	66	18	16
New Zealand 1951 §	67	15	18
United States 1940 †	68	14	18
United Kingdom 1931 †	77	17	6

mula are often unavailable and are rarely available for dates before 1930. Highly probable decision-audience values, however, may be estimated from less adequate data.

It will be noted that the principal variable in the preferred formula is *ag*, the agricultural component of a working force. Since this ranges over practically the entire percentage scale from 0 to 100, while the range of the other variable, *ac* (the autonomic component outside agriculture), is much more restricted, a rough estimate of a decision-audience value may be made from *ag* alone. Rounded to integers, the average value of *ac* in Tables 1 and 2 is 16 with a standard deviation of 5. Most of the decision-audience values in Tables 1 and 2 could have been computed without much error merely by assuming a value of 16 for *ac*. This procedure may be used to estimate probable decision-audience values. The value 16 for *ac* may be replaced by a more probable one when there is evidence pointing to a different figure, such as a computation by the preferred method for the same population at some other date.

There are, for instance, no data in Tables 1 and 2 for France, Greece, India, and the U.S.S.R. French data published in the United Nations *Demographic Yearbook* before the 1964 number are not comparable with those for other countries because assisting spouses are included in the self-employed and other unpaid family workers are grouped with paid employees. However, data are available for the agricultural component of the French working force. The percent-

---

*Except that the agricultural data used were industrial rather than occupational, these values were computed in the same way as those in Table 1. See note * to Table 1.

†Data from Table 12, 1948 number, *Demographic Yearbook*.

‡Data from Table 13, 1949–50 number, *ibid.*

§Data from Table 16, 1955 number, *ibid.*

age is 36 for 1946 and 27 for 1954.[7] Thus, if *ac* is assumed to be 16, *da's* of 48 and 57 could be estimated. However, a larger value for *ac* is suggested because the exceptionally large body of petty enterprisers in commercial distribution in France (frequently husband and wife teams) has been commented upon since far back in the nineteenth century. If one took the largest *ac* value in Tables 1 and 2 for a normal case, 27 for Belgium, *da*'s for France would be estimated as 37 for 1946 and 46 for 1954. The actual figures by the preferred formula for France in 1962 are *da* 61, *ac* 18, *ag* 21.[8] It is probable that the relatively moderate value for *ac* is a very recent development in the French economy. Given *ag* 48 for Greece in 1951, on the assumption of *ac* 16, *da* is estimated as 36 for that year.[9] Values by the preferred formula for Greece in 1961 were *da* 25, *ac* 21, *ag* 54.[10] Although some decline in *da* seems to have occurred in this case, it was probably less than is here indicated, since a value greater than 16 for *ac* in 1951 is suggested by the later data. Given *ag* 71 for India in 1951 and allowing 16 for *ac* gives an estimated *da* for that year of 13.[11] For 1961 the preferred formula gives *da* as 11 on the basis of *ag* 73 and *ac* 16 (per data).[12] For the Soviet Union the working force in agriculture has been given as 61 per cent for 1937.[13] In view of the socialist economy, it may be assumed that the number of self-employed persons and unpaid family workers

[7]Table 13, 1949–1950 number, and Table 12, 1956 number, *Demographic Yearbook,* respectively. The drop in this figure from 1946 to 1954 is exaggerated by a change in census procedure.

[8]Table 13, 1964 number, *ibid.*

[9]Table 12, 1956 number, *ibid.*

[10]Table 13, 1964 number, *ibid.*

[11]Table 15, 1956 number, *ibid.*

[12]Table 12, 1964 number, *ibid.*

[13]Data attributed to official sources, S. N. Harper and R. Thompson, *The Government of the Soviet Union* (New York, 1952), p. 178.

outside agriculture was negligible by 1937 in that country.[14] Thus, *ac* can be taken to be 0 and *da* appears to be 39.

COMPOSITION OF A DECISION-AUDIENCE—PREFERRED METHOD OF ANALYSIS

Most of the data (24 items) used in Table 1 are so classified as to allow a close estimate of the occupational categories making up the decision-audiences.[15] In these cases, most of the categories consisting largely of autonomics may be readily excluded, leaving a residue that must be closely representative of the composition of the decision-audience. The preferred procedure for estimating the composition of a decision-audience has been adopted with the possibilities of this specific body of data in mind. It involves distributing the data between a category "largely autonomics" and a category "largely members of the decision-audience" as follows:

Occupational classes in data	*Largely autonomics*	*Largely members of the decision-audience*
1. Professional, technical, etc.	none	all
2. Managerial, administrative, clerical, etc.	self-employed and unpaid family workers	paid employees
3. Sales personnel	none	all
4. Farmers, fishermen, hunters, lumbermen, etc.	all	none

[14]There were, of course, some members of producer co-operatives, and these occasionally occur in occupational statistics for several other countries in very recent years. In legal status they are similar to self-employed persons. Given an enterprise of any size, however, their sociological status within the firm is more analogous for our purposes to that of paid employees. In those recent cases in which figures for members of producer co-operatives appear separately, we have added them to paid employees.

[15]This is true of the data from Table 15, 1956 number, *Demographic Yearbook*. The data from Table 12 of the 1948 number (6 cases) are not suitably classified.

5. Workers in mines, quarries, etc.	one and one-half the self-employed plus unpaid family workers	paid employees less one-half the self-employed
6. Workers in operating transport occupations		
7. Craftsmen, production workers, and laborers not otherwise classified		
8. Service workers		
9. Not elsewhere classified		
10. Armed forces (if separately shown)[16]	none	all

The grouping "largely members of the decision-audience" is larger than the true decision-audience as earlier defined, since it does not exclude the minor categories (especially in data classes 6, 7, and 8) that are presumably autonomic by virtue of the nature of their specific occupational tasks. As a proportion of the whole working force, it is always a higher percentage than the decision-audience value computed under the preferred formula because of the treatment of data classes 1, 2, and 3 in the distribution.[17] While the true decision-audience must be slightly smaller than the category here used to represent it, there is no ground for saying whether it is greater or less than the computed decision-audience value. This also does not exclude from the decision-audience minor occupational categories that are necessarily autonomic but, on the other hand, it does not specifically include professional, ad-

[16]This category was usually not clearly shown in the censuses on which Table 1 was based. If enumerated at all, armed forces were likely to be included with service workers. For uniformity, they were added to that item in those cases where they were separately enumerated in constructing Table 3. Later data published in the 1964 number, *Demographic Yearbook* more commonly show the armed forces as a distinct category. Where this is true, they have been treated as here indicated. Several modifications in the phraseology of classifications here given appear in more recent data in the *Demographic Yearbook*. There should, however, be no difficulty in recognizing the categories referred to.

[17]The discrepancy varies from 2 to 10 per cent of the total working force in the 24 cases.

ministrative, clerical, and sales personnel in the decision-audience, as is done in the present procedure.

As has been indicated earlier, a decision-audience may be considered to be divided into a nonmanual portion and a manual portion. The importance of this distinction arises from the different ways in which the basic characteristic of the members of the decision-audience—their attention to the decisions of other persons (roughly their orientation to social rather than to material data)—may be embodied in an established pattern of cultural values. In principle, the members of the nonmanual portion of a decision-audience are either engaged in, or closely associated with, authoritative, directive, and managerial activities. Their working roles may, therefore, be related readily to values imputed to the society as a whole. They may easily adopt a cultural orientation that appears to be constructive, altruistic, and work-oriented. In principle, this is not the case for members of the manual portion of a decision-audience. For the most part, manual workers belonging to the decision-audience are socially isolated from persons engaged in authoritative, directive, and managerial activities and may themselves have no real opportunities for constructive decision-making with regard to the working operations in which they engage. Their cultural orientation toward their work, therefore, is almost necessarily class-centered and consciously resistant to the definitions of status and roles accepted by those in more authoritative social positions.

In analyzing the composition of an actual decision-audience, it is fairly clear that, in the sense just defined, the nonmanual decision-audience includes most persons enumerated in data classes 1, 2, and 3 above, which will be called the "white-collar component," and that the manual decision-audience includes most persons enumerated in data classes

5 and 7. Only the latter classes will be enumerated as the manual decision-audience. Data classes 6, 8, and 9 comprise a more varied category. Presumably the situation of members in these classes varies in the degree to which they may readily identify with the established social order and with its leading personnel. Members of these data classes will be called the "services component." For practical purposes, they will be grouped along with the white-collar component as making up the nonmanual decision-audience. Thus, in practice, a strict definition is used for the manual decision-audience and a loose definition for the nonmanual decision-audience.

DECISION-AUDIENCE COMPOSITIONS ANALYZED BY THE PREFERRED METHOD

Table 3 shows the percentage distribution among the manual-labor component, the services component, and the white-collar component of the members of the twenty-four decision-audiences represented in Table 1 for which data are classified so as to allow analysis by the preferred method. The items are listed according to the computed decision-audience values shown for the same working forces in Table 1 in the order from lowest to highest.

FOUR LEVELS OF DEVELOPMENT DISTINGUISHED BY THE COMPOSITION OF THE WORKING FORCE

Table 3 shows a patterned variance of the internal composition of working forces when these are ranged according to decision-audience values. As the decision-audience increases as a percentage of the working force, the manual portion of the decision-audience first increases gradually, reaching somewhat less than half of the decision-audience when the latter is over half the working force, and then declines as

Table 3. Percentage distribution of twenty-four decision-audiences among manual-labor, services, and white-collar components*

Country and date	Computed decision-audience value (per Table 1)	Manual-labor portion	Services portion	White-collar portion
Pakistan 1951	2	0	23	77
Thailand 1947	4	8	50	42
Haiti 1950	5	12	37	51
Honduras 1950	8	30	35	35
Guatemala 1950	15	27	37	36
Paraguay 1950	20	24	42	34
El Salvador 1950	22	36	38	26
Ecuador 1950	32	54	23	23
Japan 1950	32	36	9	55
Panama 1950	32	27	36	37
Costa Rica 1950	33	36	31	33
Venezuela 1950	37	35	38	27
Cuba 1953	40	36	24	40
Chile 1952	45	40	32	28
Finland 1950	46	42	25	33
Israel 1948	51	39	12	49
Austria 1951	52	48	22	30
Denmark 1950	57	39	24	37
Sweden 1950	67	47	17	36
Canada 1951	68	42	18	40
Australia 1947	69	—†	—‡	38
New Zealand 1945	69	34	27	39
United States 1950	74	40	20	40
United Kingdom 1951	86	35	33	32

*All data are from Table 15, 1956 number, *Demographic Yearbook.*
†Data not suitably classified: less than 49 per cent.
‡Data not suitably classified: greater than 13 per cent.

a percentage of the decision-audience while the latter continues to increase.[18] While the data refer to different coun-

[18]This may be made clear by a running average of three based on the column in Table 3 showing the manual-labor portion of the decision-audience. Two slight interruptions of the trends are produced by the aberrant values for Ecuador and Denmark. If these are eliminated, the running average produces a series of 19 values. The first 16 are increasing or constant. The last 4 are decreasing. The turning value is 46, corresponding to empirical 47 for Sweden at *da* 67.

tries, the general shape suggests a developmental pattern through which the working force of a particular polity might be expected to pass in the course of socioeconomic development. Table 3 can be interpreted according to a concept of four levels of socioeconomic development.

At Level 1 practically all productive labor other than the provision of personal services takes place in the context of peasant agriculture or of family artisan enterprise. There is thus practically no manual decision-audience and little need for the governing, directive, and coordinative activities which occupy members of a nonmanual decision-audience. Much of the little governmental and coordinative economic activity required is supplied sporadically on a part-time basis by members either of the autonomic component or of a leisured aristocracy that is outside the working force. A small body of professional, clerical, and service personnel may, however, make up a strictly minimal nonmanual decision-audience.

At Level 2 a very small manual decision-audience—consisting largely of personnel drawn from, and retaining contacts with, the autonomic component—marks a more urbanized condition. Lacking cogent responsibilities analogous to those of peasants and independent artisans, they are at least potentially a source of insurrectionary personnel. The polity must now be policed and managed. Some body of persons must necessarily be engaged regularly in such functions or at least in clerical tasks ancillary thereto. The nonmanual decision-audience thus also constitutes an appreciable portion of the working force.

At Level 3 the manual decision-audience has expanded to the point where it constitutes a self-perpetuating social formation, tending to transmit within itself a distinct cultural tradition. Although the nonmanual decision-audience has also expanded, it is still small enough so that its cultural influence does not permeate the other working force components.

At Level 4 the nonmanual decision-audience has become so large that with even moderate social mobility, family relationships bring members of the three components together to such a degree that cultural lines between them are indistinct and essentially lacking.

Thus, the postulated distinctions among the levels relate to cultural divisions within a population which in turn rest on occupational and status divisions. In a society at Level 1 there is essentially one single culture group within the working population, although a leisured aristocracy may be present and will then constitute a distinct culture group. At Level 2 there are two distinct culture groups within the working force. One of these embraces the dominant personnel of the society and extends to a significant degree through much of the nonmanual decision-audience. The other culture group embraces the autonomic component and tends to include the only slightly differentiated manual decision-audience. At Level 3 there are three distinct culture groups within the working force: the autonomic component, the manual decision-audience, and the nonmanual decision-audience. At Level 4 there are no longer distinct culture groups within the working force, the culture of the nonmanual decision-audience having largely extended through the other two components.

It is postulated that the typical conditions of each level are associated[19] with numerical values of working-force composition as follows:

[19]Because of the obvious lack of strict comparability of the raw data from which our values are computed, we state such associations as these as far as possible roughly in decile values (10 per cent, 30 per cent, 40 per cent, etc.). The evidence for such associations can be presented only

Level 1—manual decision-audience 0 per cent of the working force.

Level 2—manual decision-audience 4 to 6 per cent of the working force.

Level 3—manual decision-audience not less than 10 per cent of the working force, nonmanual decision-audience less than 30 per cent of the working force.

Level 4—nonmanual decision-audience not less than 40 per cent of the working force.

The entries in Table 3 may be rearranged by levels as shown in Table 4. Note that the manual decision-audience and the nonmanual decision-audience are here shown as percentages of the total working force rather than of the decision-audience alone as in Table 3.

Since data for the analysis of the internal composition of a decision-audience by the preferred method are often unavailable, a decision-audience value will often have to be taken as the best available indication of the level of development a population has reached. The following conventional identification of ranges of decision-audience values with levels seems to be reliable in most cases:

Level	da *range*
1	0–4
Transitional 1 to 2	5–9
2	10–19
Transitional 2 to 3	20–29
3	30–49
Transitional 3 to 4	50–69
4	70–

in the context of the total theory. See Chapter III. Identified in this way, the levels have verifiable theoretical consequences in the development of political systems.

Table 4. The twenty-four working forces of Table 3 distributed among four postulated levels of development

Country and date	Decision-audience value	Percentage of working force: In autonomic component	In manual decision-audience	In nonmanual decision-audience
Level 1				
Pakistan 1951	2	98	0	2
Thailand 1947	4	96	0	4
Transitional: Level 1 to Level 2				
Haiti 1950	5	95	1	4
Honduras 1950	8	92	2	6
Level 2				
Guatemala 1950	15	85	4	11
Paraguay 1950	20	80	5	15
Transitional: Level 2 to Level 3				
El Salvador 1950	22	78	8	14
Panama 1950	32	68	9	23
Level 3				
Ecuador 1950	32	68	17	15
Japan 1950	32	68	12	20
Costa Rica 1950	33	67	12	21
Venezuela 1950	37	63	13	24
Cuba 1953	40	60	14	26
Chile 1952	45	55	18	27
Finland 1950	46	54	19	27
Austria 1951	52	48	25	27
Transitional: Level 3 to Level 4				
Israel 1948	51	49	20	31
Denmark 1950	57	43	22	35
Sweden 1950	67	33	31	36
Canada 1951	68	32	29	39
Australia 1947	69	31	—	—*
Level 4				
New Zealand 1945	69	31	23	46
United States 1950	74	26	30	44
United Kingdom 1951	86	14	30	56

*This value cannot be exactly determined. It is somewhat more than 35.

It will be noted that Table 4 shows four items that depart from these conventional ranges. In three of these cases (Paraguay, Panama, and New Zealand) a change of one point in one of the relevant values (either *da* or the criterial value for the level) would remove the discrepancy. A change of three points in the other case (Austria) would remove the discrepancy. In view of the rather obvious lack of comparability of the relevant data within such narrow ranges, it is pointless to seek a closer fit by specifying less regular conventional divisions in the scale.

THE ESTIMATION OF THE COMPOSITION OF A DECISION-AUDIENCE

Just as data that permit the computation of a decision-audience value by the preferred formula are seldom available for earlier periods, so they are almost never available suitably classified by occupation and status for earlier periods so as to permit an analysis of the internal composition of a decision-audience under the preferred method used in Tables 3 and 4. Fortunately, however, the distribution of members of a decision-audience between the manual and the nonmanual portion is closely related to the industrial distribution of the nonagricultural working force as between industrial production and other activities. Table 5 compares percentages of the decision-audience shown as in the manual portion in Table 3 with the ratio of workers in the industrial categories "mines and quarries," "industry" (or "manufacture"), and "construction" to the total nonagricultural working force. The items consist of the eighteen cases included in Table 3 that are also shown according to an industrial classification in the United Nations *Demographic Yearbook.*

Except for the three cases of lowest decision-audience values (all below 10), there are only two cases (Finland and the United Kingdom) in Table 5 where the percentages compared vary by more than five.

Table 5. A comparison of the manual portion of the decision-audience with the industrial portion of the nonagricultural working force

Country and date	Decision-audience value (Table 1)	Manual portion of decision-audience (Table 3)	Ratio of mines and quarries, industry, and construction to nonagricultural working force (industrial basis) *
Pakistan 1951	2	0	31
Haiti 1950	5	12	33
Honduras 1950	8	30	44
El Salvador 1950	22	36	40
Ecuador 1950	32	54	52
Panama 1950	32	27	23
Costa Rica 1950	33	36	35
Venezuela 1950	37	35	31
Chile 1952	45	40	41
Finland 1950	46	42	50
Austria 1951	52	48	53
Denmark 1950	57	39	44
Sweden 1950	67	47	50
Canada 1951	68	42	43
Australia 1947	69	—†	42
New Zealand 1945	69	34	35
United States 1950	74	40	40
United Kingdom 1951	86	35	50

*All data from Table 16, 1955 number, *Demographic Yearbook.*
†Data not suitably classified: less than 49 per cent.

Evidently the industrial proportion of the nonagricultural working force may be taken as a fairly reliable indicator of the size of the manual portion of the decision-audience when the decision-audience value is not extremely low or (perhaps) extremely high. This means of estimating will be used to show that in certain historical cases the development of the internal composition of the decision-audience followed the general pattern suggested in Table 3.

It will be noted that the industrial proportion of the non-agricultural working force is entirely misleading as an indication of the manual portion of the decision-audience in the case of the working forces with the three lowest decision-audience values. This is to be expected since at this level practically all industrial production, and manual labor in general, takes place within the autonomic component rather than the decision-audience.

HISTORICAL DEVELOPMENT OF WORKING FORCES

Use of the method for estimating decision-audience value by assuming a value (usually 16) for *ac* and of the method for estimating the composition of a decision-audience by assuming that manual is to total decision-audience as the category "mining, manufacturing, and construction" is to total non-agricultural working force allows an approximate reconstruction of the past history of several working forces from available data. For eleven countries it has been possible to construct probable time-series on this basis and so to give some indication of progress from level to level. The time-series so constructed range from 140 years for the United States down to 51 years for Germany. These are portrayed diagrammatically in Figures 2 to 12 in order according to the number of years covered. In these diagrams the vertical measure represents percentage of working force. The lower curve measures the nonmanual decision audience, the higher curve the decision-audience as a whole (i.e., decision-audience value). The horizontal measure represents elapsed time, and all diagrams run from 1820 to 1960, although data fully cover this period only for the United States. Thus, the space below the lower curve graphically represents the growth of the non-manual decision-audience over time. The space between the two curves likewise shows the growth of the manual decision-audience. The space above the higher curve represents the decline over time of the autonomic component (including agriculture). Horizontal lines have been drawn to set off the portions of each diagram representing time elapsed at each one of the four levels, and such levels are indicated in the upper margin. To facilitate comparison of the several diagrams, Figure 1 has been constructed to show, in the

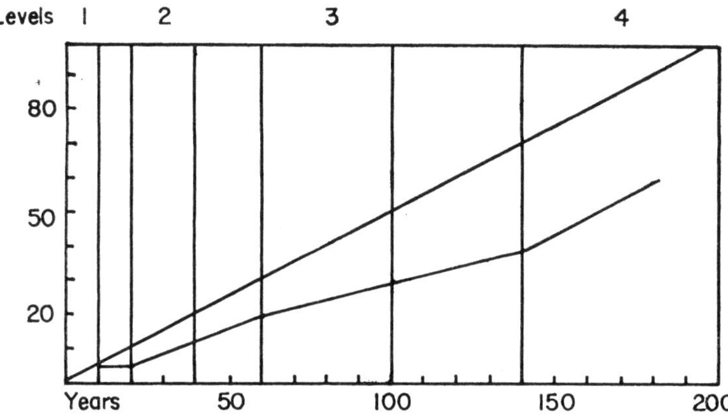

Figure 1. Hypothetical working force development through all levels, for comparison with Figures 2–12. For each of the figures, the vertical measure represents percentage of working force; the horizontal, elapsed time. The lower curve measures nonmanual decision-audience; the higher curve, decision-audience as a whole (i.e., decision-audience value).

same form as the other diagrams, a hypothetical development through all four levels on the assumption of a steady increase of decision-audience value from 0 to 100 over a period of 200 years. (The extreme values in Figure 1 may well be nonempirical.)

Figure 2 shows the development of the United States working force from 1820 to 1960. The initial condition is Level 2.[20] The transition to Level 3 begins about 1825. Level 3

[20]Throughout this section, in the interests of style, we are flatly stating what the data, as interpreted, show. The reader should be aware that percentages used and dates of change among levels are merely more or less probable.

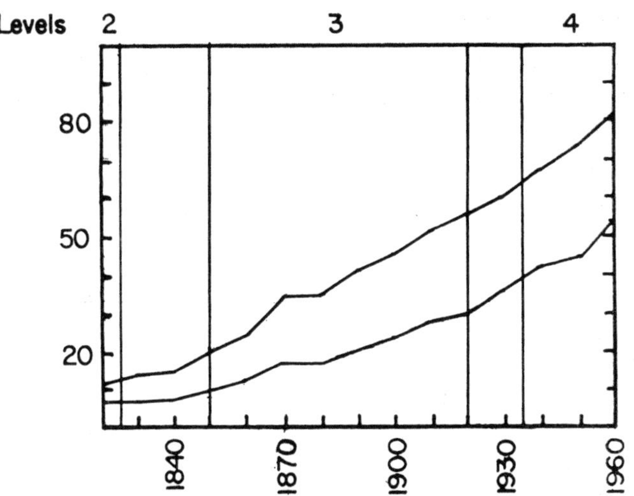

Figure 2. Working force development: The United States. For an explanation of the measures, see Figure 1.

begins about 1850 and lasts until 1920. Level 4 begins about 1935. Values plotted in Figure 2 are the following:[21]

Date	*Decision-audience value* (da)	*Nonmanual decision-audience as percentage of working force*
1820	12	7
1830	14	7
1840	15	8
1850	20	10
1860	25	13
1870	34	17

[21]Data for 1820 through 1940 are from United States, *Historical Statistics of the United States* (Washington, 1960), p. 74, series 57–71. This is an industrial classification and values are estimated by the usual procedures. Values for 1950 are those of Table 4. Values for 1960 are computed by the preferred method from data in Table 13, 1964 number, *Demographic Yearbook.*

1880	34	17
1890	41	21
1900	46	24
1910	52	28
1920	57	30
1930	60	36
1940	67	42
1950	74	44
1960	81	54

Figure 3 shows the development of the British working force from 1841 to 1951. The initial condition is Level 3,

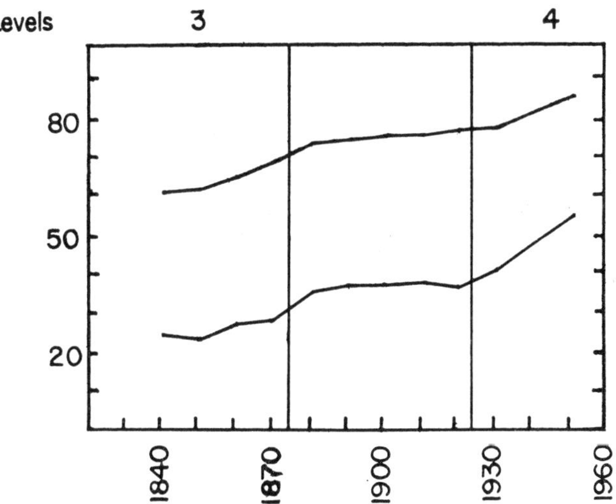

Figure 3. Working force development: The United Kingdom. For an explanation of the measures, see Figure 1.

which continues until about 1875. Level 4 is attained about 1925. The values plotted in Figure 3 are the following:[22]

[22]The values for 1951 are those in Table 4. Values for the earlier years are estimated by the usual methods from percentage distributions of the working force in Colin Clark, *The Conditions of Economic Progress* (London, 1940), p. 187. The jump in nonmanual decision-audience from 1931 to 1951 is presumably exaggerated. The method for estimating the earlier figures would give 43 for 1951. The true value for 1931 was probably above 41.

Date	*Decision-audience value* (da)	*Nonmanual decision-audience as percentage of working force*
1841	61	26
1851	62	24
1861	65	27
1871	69	29
1881	73	37
1891	74	38
1901	76	38
1911	76	38
1921	77	37
1931	78	41
1951	86	56

Figure 4 shows the development of the Australian working force from 1871 to 1961. The initial condition is Level 3. The

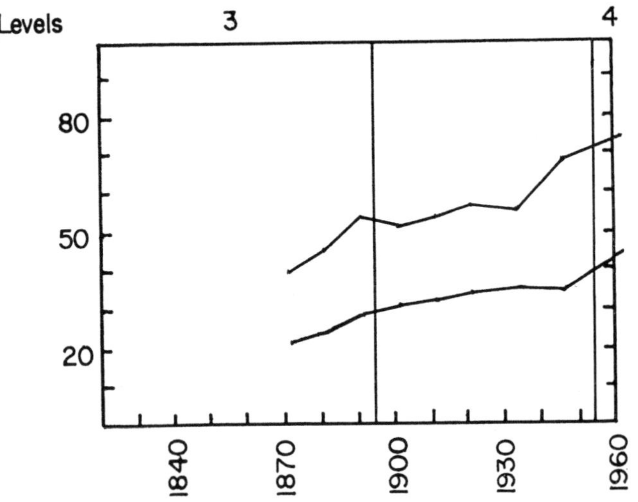

Figure 4. Working force development: Australia. For an explanation of the measures, see Figure 1.

transition to Level 4 begins about 1895. Level 4 is attained about 1955. Values plotted in Figure 4 are the following:[23]

Date	*Decision-audience value* (da)	*Nonmanual decision-audience as percentage of working force*
1871	40	21
1881	46	24
1891	53	29
1901	51	31
1911	54	32
1921	58	34
1933	57	36
1947	69	35
1961	74	43

Figure 5 shows the development of the Swedish working force from 1870 to 1960. The initial date seems to mark the termination of Level 2. Level 3 begins about 1885. The transition from Level 3 to Level 4 begins about 1948. Level 4 is attained about 1955. The values plotted in Figure 5[24] are

[23]Data from 1881 through 1933 are from Clark, *ibid.,* p. 194. Values are estimated by usual procedures. The 1947 values are those of Table 4. The value 35 for nonmanual decision-audience in 1947 is somewhat too low since transportation was included with industry in data. The 1961 *da* is computed by the preferred method and the 1961 nonmanual decision-audience is estimated by the usual procedures from data (industrial) in Table 12, 1964 number, *Demographic Yearbook.*

[24]The values for 1950 are those of Table 4. Those for 1960 are derived by the preferred method from data in Table 13, 1964 number, *Demographic Yearbook.* Data for the earlier years are the percentage distributions of the working force in W. S. Wotinsky and E. S. Wotinsky, *World Population and Production* (New York, 1953), p. 356. Plotted values were estimated from these data by the usual procedures.

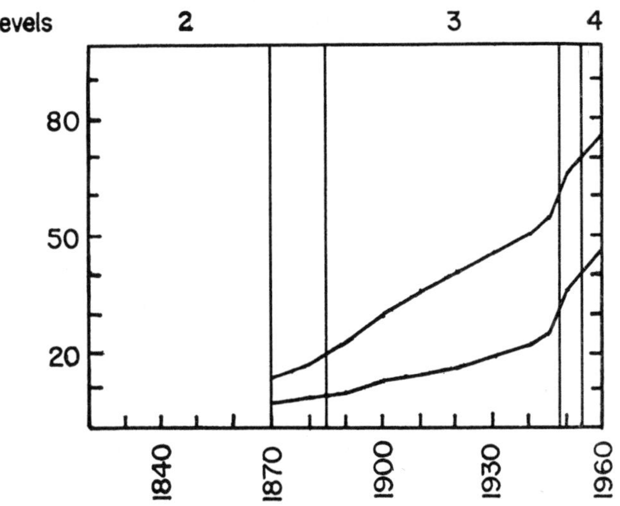

Figure 5. Working force development: Sweden. For an explanation of the measures, see Figure 1.

the following:

Date	*Decision-audience value* (da)	*Nonmanual decision-audience as percentage of working force*
1870	12	6
1880	16	8
1890	22	9
1900	29	11
1910	35	13
1920	40	15
1930	45	18
1940	50	21
1945	54	23
1950	67	36
1960	75	45

Figure 6 shows the development of the Japanese working force from 1872 to 1960. The condition is Level 1 at the beginning of the record. The transition from Level 1 to Level

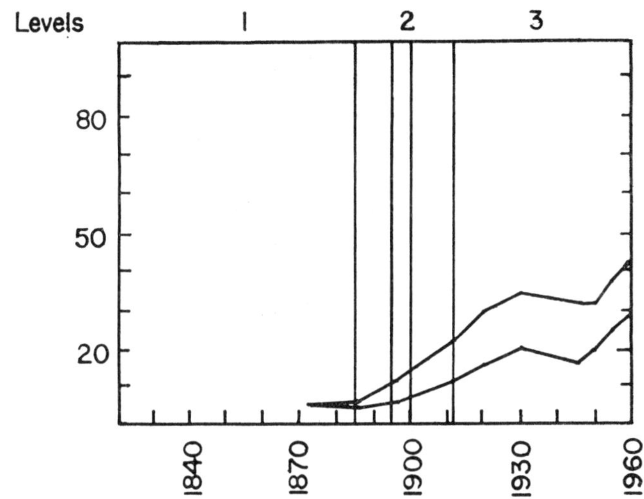

Figure 6. Working force development: Japan. For an explanation of the measures, see Figure 1.

2 takes about ten years from 1885 to 1895. The Level 2 condition ends about 1900. Level 3 begins about 1912. The Level 3 condition has not quite been surpassed in 1960. The values plotted in Figure 6 are the following:[25]

[25]The 1950 values are those of Table 4. Those for 1955 and 1960 are derived by the preferred method from data in Table 13, 1964 number, *Demographic Yearbook*. The 1947 data are in Wotinsky, *op. cit.*, p. 357. Earlier data are in Clark, *op. cit.*, p. 192. Values for the dates 1897 through 1947 were estimated by the usual procedures. The level of development in 1872 is too low for estimating either *da* or the internal composition of the decision-audience by the usual procedures. We used the percentage in data for public administration, professions, and domestic service for *da* and nonmanual *da* in 1872 and for nonmanual *da* in 1887. For that year *da* is estimated by the usual method.

Date	*Decision-audience value* (da)	*Nonmanual decision-audience as percentage of working force*
1872	4	4
1887	6	5
1897	12	6
1912	22	12
1920	30	16
1930	34	20
1947	32	17
1950	32	20
1955	38	25
1960	47	29

Figure 7 shows the development of the Italian working force from 1871 to 1959. The condition is Level 3 through-

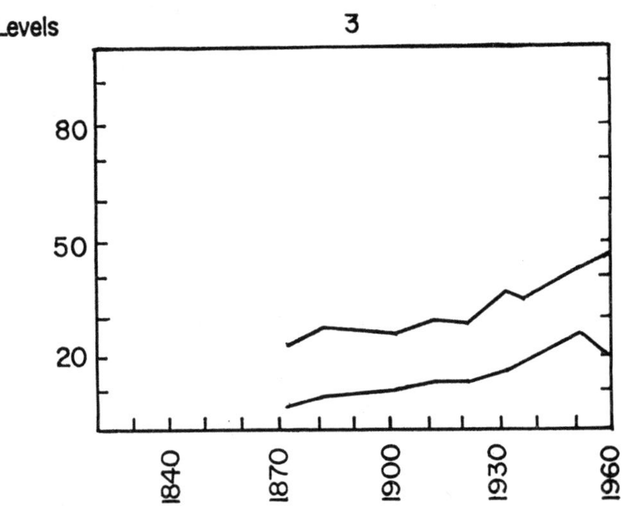

Figure 7. Working force development: Italy. For an explanation of the measures, see Figure 1.

out. Values plotted in Figure 7 are the following:[26]

Date	*Decision-audience value* (da)	*Nonmanual decision-audience as percentage of working force*
1871	22	7
1881	27	9
1901	25	10
1911	29	12
1921	28	12
1931	37	16
1936	33	—
1951	42	25
1959	46	20

Figure 8 shows the development of the Swiss working force

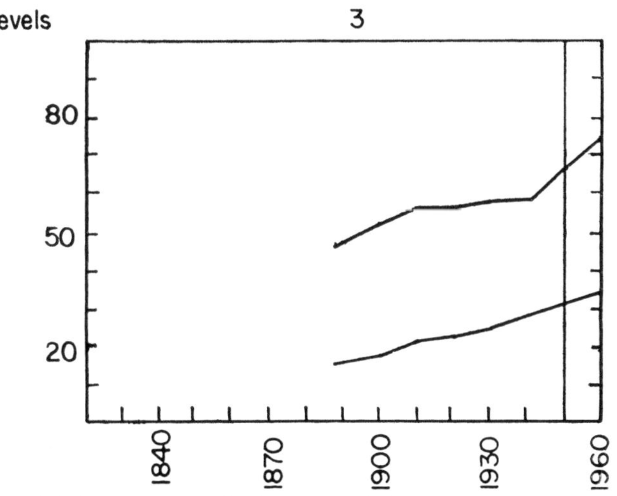

Figure 8. Working force development: Switzerland. For an explanation of the measures, see Figure 1.

[26]Data for 1871 through 1931 are from Clark, *ibid.*, p. 201. Values are

from 1888 to 1960. The condition is Level 3 until about 1950. Values plotted in Figure 8 are the following:[27]

Date	*Decision-audience value* (da)	*Nonmanual decision-audience as percentage of working force*
1888	46	16
1900	52	18
1910	57	21
1920	57	22
1930	58	24
1941	59	—
1950	66	—
1960	74	33

Figure 9 shows the development of the Canadian working force. The condition is Level 3 until about 1931 and Level

---

estimated by the usual procedures. The 1936 *da* is that in Table 2. The 1951 values are estimated by the usual procedures from data in Table 12, 1956 number, *Demographic Yearbook.* The 1959 values are computed from data in Italy, *Annuario Statistico Italiano 1959* (Rome, 1960), pp. 314–315.

[27]Values for 1888 through 1930 are estimated by the usual procedures (except that in 1930 20, the value in 1941, is assumed for *ac* rather than 16) from data in Clark, *op. cit.,* p. 198. For 1941 and 1950 *da* is computed by the preferred method from data in Table 12, 1948 number, and Table 16, 1955 number, *Demographic Yearbook,* respectively. For 1960 *da* is computed by the preferred method and nonmanual decision-audience is estimated by the usual procedures from data (industrial) in Table 12, 1964 number, *ibid.*

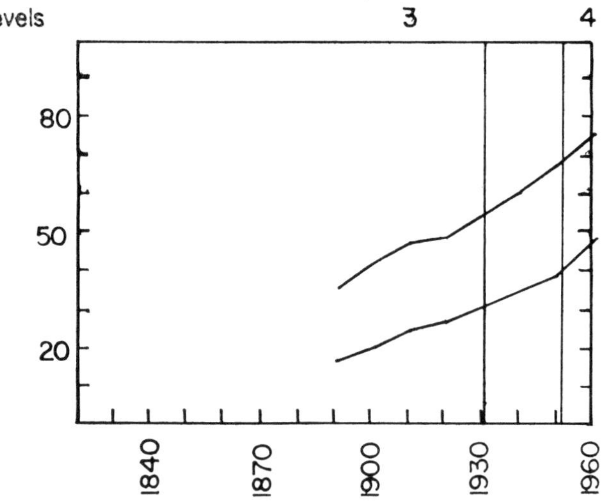

Figure 9. Working force development: Canada. For an explanation of the measures, see Figure 1.

4 after about 1952. Values plotted in Figure 9 are the following:[28]

Date	*Decision-audience value* (da)	*Nonmanual decision-audience as percentage of working force*
1891	36	17
1901	42	20
1911	47	23
1921	49	27

[28]Values for 1891 through 1931 are estimated by the usual procedures from data in Clark, *op. cit.*, p. 194. For 1941 *da* is computed by the preferred method from data in Table 12, 1948 number, *Demographic Yearbook.* For 1951 and 1961 values are computed by the preferred methods from data in Table 15, 1956 number, and Table 13, 1964 number, *ibid.*, respectively.

1931	53	30
1941	60	—
1951	68	39
1961	75	49

Figure 10 shows the development of the Norwegian working force from 1891 to 1960. The initial condition is Level 3, which lasts until about 1935. Level 4 is attained about 1955.[29]

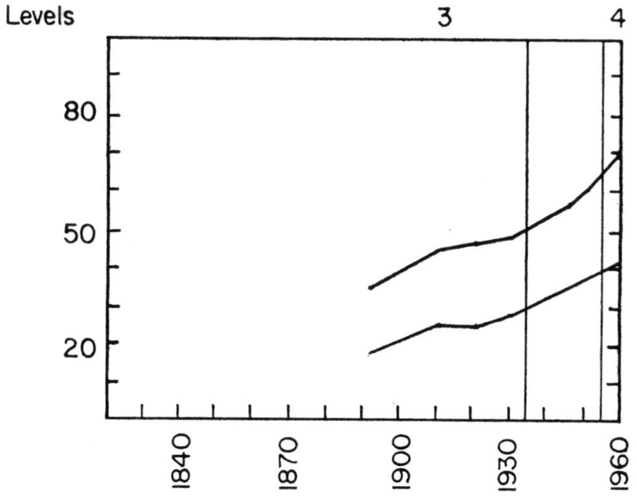

Figure 10. Working force development: Norway. For an explanation of the measures, see Figure 1.

[29]Values for 1891 through 1930 are estimated by the usual procedures (except that for 1930 14, the value for 1946 and for 1950, is assumed for *ac* instead of 16) from data in Clark, *op. cit.,* p. 203. The *da*'s for 1946 and 1950 and the values for 1960 are computed by the preferred methods from data in Table 12, 1948 number, Table 16, 1955 number, and Table 13, 1964 number, *Demographic Yearbook,* respectively.

Date	*Decision-audience value* (da)	*Nonmanual decision-audience as percentage of working force*
1891	34	18
1910	44	25
1920	47	25
1930	48	28
1946	57	—
1950	60	—
1960	69	41

Figure 11 shows the development of the Danish working force from 1901 to 1960. The condition is Level 3 until about

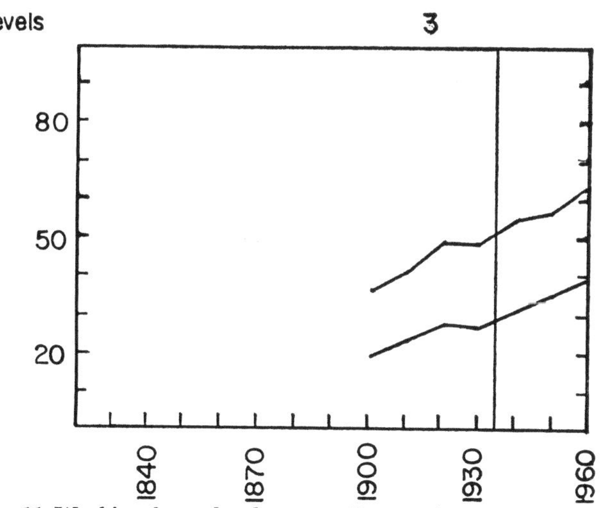

Figure 11. Working force development: Denmark. For an explanation of the measures, see Figure 1.

1935. Level 4 has not quite been attained in 1960. The values plotted in Figure 11 are the following:[30]

[30]Values for 1901 through 1930 are estimated by the usual procedures

Date	*Decision-audience value* (da)	*Nonmanual decision-audience as percentage of working force*
1901	36	19
1911	41	23
1921	49	28
1930	48	27
1940	54	—
1950	57	35
1960	64	39

Figure 12 shows the development of the German workin force from 1882 through 1933. The condition is Level 3 unti

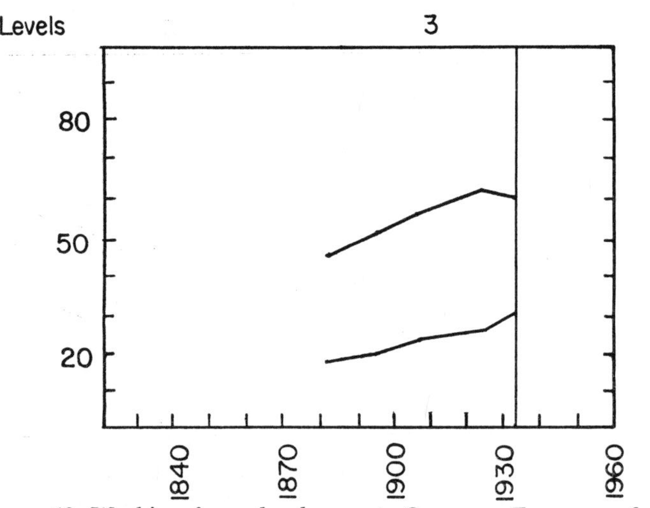

Figure 12. Working force development: Germany. For an explana tion of the measures, see Figure 1.

---

from data in Clark, *op. cit.*, p. 196. The *da* for 1940 and the values fc 1950 and 1960 are computed by the preferred method from data i Table 12, 1948 number, Table 15, 1956 number, and Table 13, 196 number, *Demographic Yearbook,* respectively.

1933. Data plotted in Figure 12 are the following:[31]

Date	*Decision-audience value* (da)	*Nonmanual decision-audience as percentage of working force*
1882	45	18
1895	51	20
1907	57	23
1925	62	25
1933	60	30

Approximate transitional dates, as indicated in Figures 2–12, may be recapitulated as follows:

Start of transition from Level 1 to Level 2:
- Japan 1885

Start of Level 2:
- Japan 1895

Start of transition from Level 2 to Level 3:
- United States 1825
- Sweden 1870
- Japan 1900

Start of Level 3:
- United States 1850
- Sweden 1885
- Japan 1912

Start of transition from Level 3 to Level 4:
- United Kingdom 1875
- Australia 1895
- United States 1920

[31] Data are from Clark, *op. cit.*, p. 190. Values are estimated by the usual procedures.

Canada 1931
Germany 1933
Denmark 1935
Norway 1935
Sweden 1948
Switzerland 1950

Start of Level 4:

United Kingdom 1925
United States 1935
Canada 1952
Australia 1955
Norway 1955
Sweden 1955

Approximate durations of the several stages may be of interest. The transition from Level 2 to Level 3 varied from 12 to 25 years in the three cases available; Level 3 lasted 70 years in the United States, 63 years in Sweden, and at least 50 years in Japan; and the transition from Level 3 to Level 4 lasted 60 years in Australia, 50 years in the United Kingdom, 21 years in Canada, 20 years in Norway, 15 years in the United States, and 7 years in Sweden.

CHAPTER III

The Three Types of Regimes at the Four Levels—A Historical Survey

IN THIS chapter, the political history of European nation-states and nation-states of European antecedents will be summarized for the purpose of classifying their successive regimes according to the criteria[1] set down in Chapter I and of indicating, as far as possible, the levels, as defined in Chapter II, at which these regimes occurred. The general arrangement of regime-types according to levels which this exposition will show has been sketched in Chapter I. There is, however, no statistical evidence of levels before the nineteenth century, and the kind of census evidence required for the preferred calculations of level is generally not available until the mid-twentieth century. For earlier periods, the most that can be claimed is that there is no obstacle in the gross data of history to supposing that the various types of regimes occurred before at the levels at which they can be shown to occur in recent decades, that the types of regime to which the theory refers are already clearly recognizable, and that the

[1]Criterion 20 will be used only in a section of the exposition below dealing with the stability of regimes. Otherwise it is ignored.

various types, once established, were persistent then, as they are now.

THE SEVENTEENTH CENTURY

In 1600 the only political entities closely resembling modern nation-states were the following eight: Denmark, England, France, Portugal, Russia, Scotland, Spain, and Sweden. Even then, in most of these cases, the whole area of each country cannot be treated as a single polity. There were still areas within them with some degree of local autonomy on a feudalistic or tribal basis. Highland Scotland, for instance, was little more than a series of dependencies loosely attached to the more firmly organized polity in the South. In France there were still feudal areas distinct enough to form bases for civil warfare shortly after this date, and the Protestant towns had a good deal of autonomous power. Nonetheless, in each of these cases something like a modern nationality was for the most part under a single government. Other polities of Europe were small or weakly organized or not fully independent or ethnically composite or lacked any basis for claiming to be the unique homelands of distinct and numerous peoples.

Criterion 1 is inapplicable in all eight cases. Political thought was still traditional. There were as yet no contrived and elaborated ideologies designed to have popular appeal. Hence, none could be imposed in the fashion of a utopian regime.

Criterion 2 is, of course, inapplicable because independence is one of the bases for selecting these particular polities as nation-states.

If some surviving feudalities and clan areas, such as were mentioned, are treated as distinct from the polities here analyzed, Criterion 3 was inapplicable by 1600 in all eight cases. None of these countries practiced direct democracy. None depended wholly for administration upon interconnections among locally dominant families, though this may well have been the way in which authority still reached most of the common people in rural areas. There was a complex representative structure—centering in assemblies of the "estates"—closely associated with legitimate authority in Denmark, England, Scotland, and Sweden. Similar institutions were still known locally, or vestigially on a national scale, in the other countries. In all cases there was some degree of centralized bureaucratic authority, at least in judicial or fiscal matters. Fairly bureaucratic military structures, as distinguished from feudal levies, were in some cases continuously and in others sporadically according to circumstance at the disposal of the central authorities.

Thus, none of these eight polities in 1600 had a citizen-community, a traditional, a radical-egalitarian, or a totalitarian regime. Their regimes were, therefore, necessarily main-stem other than traditional or else representative-consensual. Since all had monarchical rulers of traditional type, Criterion 4 applies and identifies them all as main-stem regimes with a right, either dichotomized or trichotomized. Criterion 7 applies in all cases, and they were thus all dichotomized regimes. For this finding (under the criterion) it is necessary only to determine that two political formations characteristic of more advanced levels of development are lacking: an important and distinct radically egalitarian left and a center mingling traditional with socially critical appeals. In Portugal, Russia, Spain, and perhaps France one cannot go beyond this in 1600 and positively identify an objective dichotomy of factions. In the other cases in 1600 or shortly thereafter, a dichotomy of recognized factional tendencies is clearly visible. In England and Scotland the political factionalism is concealed under religious forms. The extremist Presbyterian faction, which tended to dominate the Scots Lowlands through ecclesiastical administration, subsumed the socially critical position, as did the dissident Puritan religious faction in England. In these cases, a traditionalist-personalist right, associated publicly with the monarchy and the nobility, tended openly in England and covertly in Scotland to an opposing religious orientation. The traditionalist-personalist right was publicly associated with the nobility in Sweden and Denmark, the political role of the monarchies in these cases being ambiguous. In the former country the rationalist-institutionalist left appeared mainly as a peasant faction; in the latter it represented town views.

No change in regime classification in the polities mentioned occurred in the seventeenth century except in the two British countries. In the other six polities, dichotomized regimes continued with traditional monarchical forms of executive, that is, regimes to which Criteria 4 and 7 remained applicable. In Sweden the ideological dichotomy became more visible. Representative institutions were preserved because several strong monarchs, whose reigns were interspersed with regencies, found it expedient to appeal to the strongly organized and self-conscious peasant estate against the nobility as the best means of securing the mobilization of the nation's meager resources without which the spectacular Swedish military interventions abroad in this period would have been impossible. A somewhat similar line-up of forces in Denmark had a different outcome. There the peasantry was in a degraded condition and the towns could only just match the power of the nobility after the successful resistance of Copenhagen to the Swedish invasion. A movement of townspeople against the nobility eventuated after 1660 in a formally and practically absolute monarchy. In Russia, after several turbulent years at the beginning of the century, a new dynasty established its hold on power by administrative and military reforms, reasserted an already established absolutist tradition, and consolidated and expanded the national territory. In France the almost constant civil strife of the previous century continued sporadically through most of this one, being eventually overcome by more effective centralization of power in the royal administration. In the process, all representative bodies fell into disuse, and forced doctrinal conformance in religion was established in 1685 after nearly two centuries of religious division. In Spain and Portugal also the net effect of the century's developments was the emptying of real content from all political institutions other than the monarchical administration. Political history was essentially that of the Habsburg house, which in the early years of the century ruled Portugal as well as Spain, being supplanted in the smaller country by a local dynasty in the rebellion of 1640. While the net trend in all cases, with the possible exception of Sweden, was toward what is described historically as absolute monarchical rule, there was by no means a stable institutional structure in these main-stem countries throughout most of this period. To the established government the risk of rebellion by military, feudal, or regional forces could never be overlooked though, where a dynasty was well established, rebellion might require a plausible pretender to the throne. Actual uprisings were major events in France and Portugal, and serious mutinies occurred in Russia.

In contrast to the persistence of the dichotomized form of regime in the other countries, religious discord in the British polities evolved into serious factional division along lines of political principle, the collapse of normal social organization produced radical-egalitarian regimes, and the threat of renewed civil strife in a restored dichotomized regime was abated by a settlement inaugurating a representative-consensual regime.[2]

The Elizabethan religious settlement had left England with an Episcopal church organization dependent upon the royal administration and largely unaffected by the Calvinistic doctrines then spreading, particularly in artisan and mercantile circles, throughout Western Europe. In contrast, the established Presbyterian church in Scotland was Calvinistic in doctrine, and, governed through councils of clergy and select lay personnel, it dominated the more populous lowland area of the country, largely overshadowing the weakly developed royal administration.

In 1603 the King of Scotland inherited the English crown. Moving to his new kingdom to escape the control of the Presbyterians, King James I was delighted to become an enthusiastic Episcopalian as well as a dogmatic claimant of a divine right to rule. Since the King resisted any ecclesiastical changes that would have partly satisfied Calvinistic sentiment, a growing body of religious enthusiasts—the Puritans—became more and more consciously alienated in England from the established forms of both church and state.

Eventually, King James' son and successor, Charles I, was sufficiently ill-advised to seek to use the power derived from his English throne to influence Scots church practice in the direction of Episcopalianism. In 1639 the Scottish parliament,

[2]The period of the English Civil Wars is dealt with at greatest length in the writings of Samuel R. Gardiner, particularly *History of the Great Civil War, 1642–1649* (4 vols.; London, 1893), and *The First Two Stuarts and the Puritan Revolution, 1603–1660* (New York, 1895). Other general accounts include G. M. Trevelyan, *History of England,* Vol. II: *The Tudors and the Stuart Era* (Garden City, N.Y., 1953), and Winston S. Churchill, *A History of the English-Speaking Peoples,* Vol. II: *The New World* (New York, 1956). A biography of the leading protagonist of the Rebellion is Frederic Harrison, *Oliver Cromwell* (London, 1895).

regarding the King as a heretic, suspended him from his functions. A Scottish army entered England in an effort to bring his person under their control. Resisting the Scots required the support of the English parliament, which had been rarely convened in this period. As representative institutions were thus revived in England, it developed that the influential classes of the country had now become predominantly, though not overwhelmingly, Puritan. The King refused to assent to legislation that would have converted the English church from an Episcopal to a Presbyterian organization. In 1642 the English parliament followed the example of the Scots and suspended him from his office. Both sides raised armies. The "First Civil War" lasted from 1642 to 1645. At first with the aid of the Scots, later through a thoroughly professional and bureaucratized army of their own creation, the New Model, the Puritans prevailed. In the process they lost their popular support and split deeply into rival wings. The Parliament remained Presbyterian in religion and distinctly oligarchic in political sentiment. The army, which had many of the characteristics of a modern semitotalitarian dominant party, became deeply committed to the freedom of individual religious congregations from central control (what was later called "congregationalism," then "independency") and to a democratic political philosophy.

How does one reconcile a conviction that one must rule an unwilling people to save them from moral disaster and a concurrent belief that only democratic rule is legitimate? The Puritans of the New Model lacked any elaborate and sophisticated political doctrine like modern Marxist Communism, which serves to square this particular circle. Their political convictions over the next decades eventually dissolved over this dilemma. In the mean time, however, in the winter of 1648–1649 frustration released a deep-seated social convulsion. The institutional complex, such as it was,—Parliament, the army as a political movement, the independent church congregations—had become unworkable. Parliament had ordered the army dissolved. Had it been obeyed, most of the former officers and many of the troops would have been jailed as heretics. The army refused to disband—out of respect for its members' convictions as well as for their skins—but it could not make the obvious reply, a demand for a new election of parliament, since that would have restored the King to power. A consistent and principled policy being ruled out by circumstances, influence passed to those who could most unequivocally pronounce the slogans of extreme egalitarianism. Many troopers were receptive, as were mobs in the cities. The passing of authority to the extreme radicals was signalled by the seizure of the House of Commons on December 6, 1648 by a small body of troops without any ostensible authority but its own. The soldiers proceeded to send home all but a "rump" (or "sitting part") of members expected to be amenable to extremist demands.[3] The "rump" then sent home the House of Lords and established a court

[3]This action, Pride's Purge, tends to be presented as a military coup carried out by "the army" under the authority of their officers and specifically of Cromwell. We think that its political significance at the time it happened is better seen by regarding it as an informal political action of some soldiers. Although led by a Colonel and not in open mutiny, they did not claim to act on anyone's orders. Cromwell, although he had participated in consultations envisioning such an action on a hypothetical basis, was not within range of communication when the decision was precipitated by actions taken by the House. In any case, he was not yet commander-in-chief and had no formal authority over Colonel Pride's unit. The commander-in-chief, Lord Fairfax, did not order the action, though he refused requests to order it undone. See Samuel R. Gardiner, *History of the Great Civil War, 1642–1649* (London, 1893), IV, 269–272.

to try the King. He was put to death in January, 1649 in an unpopular and impolitic act.

In contrast to what later happened in similar circumstances in France in the early 1790's and in Russia in 1917, the open assertion of doctrinal extremism did not suffice wholly to dissolve the discipline of the army. The New Model was a creation of Parliament to fight the king. Its officers owed their standing and reputation largely to this rebellion. Few were holdovers from the old royalist forces. Thus, the egalitarian agitation never sufficed to drive them out and to transfer control of troops unequivocally to soldiers' committees. When in April, 1649 some portions of the New Model refused to obey orders, they were overwhelmed and severely punished by regiments loyal to the high command. Depending in the other cases on the gradual development of a new body of officers, a similar reassertion of centralized bureaucratic control of coercive power was delayed for two years in the French Revolution and for four in the Russian.

With the suppression of the mutiny in the New Model, the Puritan regime became fairly conservative in social policy. It was necessary to fight a second civil war from 1648 to 1651, in which royalist forces, now aided by the Scots, were decisively defeated. Scotland was conquered and annexed to England in 1652. The army authorities, a council of officers headed by Cromwell, became openly dominant in 1653. Cromwell under the title of lord protector held what was essentially the traditional position of king until his death in 1658. Then, faced with the prospect of indecisive strife among various portions of the army and disillusioned of previously held political principles, the effective leaders of the Puritan regime, mostly generals, after two years of maneuvering for position, invited King Charles II to return from exile in 1660.

There are six distinct regimes of the Civil War and Interregnum period to be classified. (1) The Scottish regime from 1639 to 1648, ostensibly an emanation of the Scottish parliament, rested upon the Presbyterian church administration dominating the Lowlands and on a large, fairly professional army (led in part by veterans of the continental religious wars), which was essential to ward off aristocratic and clan incursions from the North and English intervention from the South. Clearly Criteria 5 and 7 apply and the regime is dichotomized. (2) In 1648 the Scottish army was totally destroyed in England. Militant masses rose throughout the Lowlands bent upon purifying the Kirk from the upper-class heresies that had led to the unfortunate interventions in England (successively on both sides of the struggle there). Criteria 1 and 3 (the revolutionary case) apply. This radical-egalitarian regime lasted until the English conquest of Scotland in 1652.

(3) The English royalist belligerent from 1642 to its demise in 1645 is the old regime to which Criteria 4 and 7 applied. It is thus, at least initially, a dichotomized regime. As it was pushed back into less developed territory and came to depend upon more or less feudalistic levies of troops, very likely it came under Criterion 3 and thus regressed to a traditional regime. (4) The English parliamentary belligerent from 1642 to 1648 comes under Criteria 5 and 7. There was no definite political ideology prescribed and inculcated. Hence Criterion 1 is inapplicable. In the parliamentary area, most of the established administrative and military structure continued to operate. Hence Criterion 3 does not become applicable. Division of opinion and conflict of loyalties were obviously so deep that a military coup, particularly one that might lead to an accommodation with the king, was an obvious possibility much of the time. Hence Criterion 5 applies. Until the end of this regime in late 1648, there was insufficient differ-

entiation of a radical-egalitarian left to make Criterion 7 inapplicable. Thus the parliamentary belligerent, like its royalist counterpart, was a dichotomized regime.

(5) With the institutional paralysis produced by the deep disagreement between Parliament and the army offices, a large outburst of radical-egalitarian agitation occurred in late 1648, particularly in the soldiers' meetings. Pride's Purge signals the dominance of this sentiment. Criteria 1 and 3 (the revolutionary case) become applicable. The regime is then radical-egalitarian. (6) With the suppression of the mutiny in the New Model in April 1648, the leveling sentiment no longer constituted a political force and centralized administrative control was restored. Hence Criteria 1 and 3 no longer apply and the situation of a dichotomized regime is restored on the basis of the applicability of Criteria 5 and 7.

The Restoration regime, established with the recall of Charles II in 1660, was structurally the same as the regime before the Civil Wars.[4] The king was the ruler, but he could not rule effectively without the support of parliament. Criteria 4 and 7 apply as before and the regime continues to be dichotomized, as under the Puritans. In this period, the dichotomy became fairly clearly embodied in two political factions, both essentially upper-class in leadership but having followings established to some degree in the lower orders. The Tories, who dominated the government through parliament and the re-established Episcopal church, profited from the unpopularity of the late Puritan regime by professing a servile submissiveness to the king (which they did not practice) and a fixed devotion to the Episcopal religious position.

[4]For a fuller taeatment of this period, David Ogg's *England in the Reign of Charles II* (Oxford, 1934) may be suggested. The process of the restoration itself is the subject of Patrick Morrah's *The Year of Restoration* (Boston, 1961).

The Whigs constituted a second and weaker faction whose leaders refrained from identifying themselves with the current professions of the divine right of kings and thus had, or appeared to have, a following in those circles which had produced the invincible and still-feared New Model and which still consisted largely of dissenters from the Episcopal church. The Tory advantage continued to be clear until the open profession of Catholicism by King James II, who acceded in 1685, made their platform of servile royalism together with episcopalianism ridiculous. Even then Tory dominance held until the birth of an heir to the throne in 1688 made it clear that their embarrassment was not a temporary one.

The leaders of both factions recoiled from the prospect of renewed civil strife which the political-religious position of the King was now opening up. An incredibly widespread but secret conspiracy, embracing almost the whole upper class, deprived King James of his throne without permitting Englishmen to shed each other's blood over the issue. Major leaders of both factions signed a letter inviting William of Orange, the stadholder of the United Netherlands, to save the English from their King. At the moment of the consequent invasion, the large royal army was paralyzed by the concerted absence of most of its officers from their posts. William marched his token army from city to city and found each draped in orange to welcome him. Obviously, he had to be made king for his trouble—in form jointly with his wife Mary, who, as the daughter of the deposed ruler, had the somewhat better claim.

Merely for a Dutchman to usurp the English throne could not of itself have changed the nature of the regime. The regime formed by William's somewhat *pro forma* conquest of

England in the latter part of 1688 was still a dichotomized one like its predecessor. The subsequent total stability of English institutions—in the sense of immunity to coups, uprisings, and usurpations—was the result of the steps taken by the Whig and Tory leaders to formalize the new regime in the following year. The Settlement of 1689 was a mutual acceptance by previously hostile factions of each other's right to secure membership in the ruling elite. The effective guarantee lay in the fact that in the settlement, as voted by Parliament, each side violated a value with which it had been publicly identified and thus made itself incapable of reopening the struggle on a principled basis. The Tories were not permitted to avoid participation in the formal dethronement of a king and the deliberate appointment of his successor. The Whigs had to join in sponsoring a monopoly of public officeholding for Episcopalians, softened in practice but not in principle by an exemption from persecution of Protestant dissenters in general for the first time.

Thus, it was the Settlement of 1689 that created the regime that has lasted until the present day. Obviously Criteria 1, 2, and 3 do not apply to it. Criterion 4 is not applicable after 1689, since, to all reasonably informed participants, the sovereign merely held an office assigned him for the convenience of those who dominated the state, for long thereafter a very narrow oligarchy. Criterion 5 is obviously inapplicable. No army has been less political than the British. Criterion 6 does not apply since the English have no habit of routine political rioting. Thus the Settlement of 1689 created a representative-consensual regime. Though it was in no real sense democratic until the late nineteenth century, it was from the beginning a sort of "crowned republic" and utterly different from the leading monarchies of the day.

THE EIGHTEENTH CENTURY

The polities that may be considered nation-states in 1700 are the same as those listed for 1600 with the exception of Scotland, which never fully recovered complete independence after it was conquered by the English Puritans. Nominally it became a separate country again with the Restoration in 1660. Ostensibly the Glorious Revolution of 1688, changing the person occupying the English throne, merely happened to be reproduced in Scotland so that the presence of the same sovereign on the two thrones was maintained. In fact, after 1660 Scotland tended to be an English dependency, governed by appointees of the English government. However, it retained a separate parliament and a distinct established church, Presbyterian rather than Episcopalian. In 1707 England and Scotland were formally merged under the title of Great Britain with one single parliament rather than two.

As has been indicated, England in 1700 had a representative-consensual regime while Denmark, France, Portugal, Russia, Spain, and Sweden had dichotomized regimes of traditional monarchical type (Criteria 4 and 7 being applicable). All the latter polities had evolved in the preceding century toward simple centralized bureaucratic rule. The traditional representative institutions—the assemblies of estates—which had had some importance in all cases in 1600 were moribund in 1700 except in Sweden. Nothing important happened in the eighteenth century from the standpoint of our present exposition in the internal politics of Denmark, Portugal, Russia, and Spain. Criteria 4 and 7 continue to apply and these four countries continue to have dichotomized regimes. For present purposes, events in Great Britain may also be overlooked since this book is concerned not with the evolution of constitutional regimes but only with what makes them possible in the first place. Great Britain remained representative-consensual. Thus, only Sweden and France call for special attention.

A break in the dynastic succession allowed the establishment of a virtually republican constitution early in the eighteenth century in Sweden, as had earlier happened in Great Britain. Given a dichotomized regime in Sweden, however, the practical results were entirely different from those in Great Britain. An extreme rivalry of factions threatened to upset all institutions and to bring on foreign intervention besides. After a wild experience of representative politics under main-stem conditions, the century ended with a widespread acceptance of restored monarchical authority in a form that amounted to a bureaucratic-military dictatorship.

Charles XII, the last strong Swedish ruler of the seventeenth-century line, died in 1718 without a clear successor.[5] The estates first elected his sister to the royal office and then, on her abdication in 1720, elected her husband to a largely nominal kingship. All power was vested in the quadricameral estates: nobles, priests, burgesses, peasants. Any three could enact law. During sessions of the estates, a "secret committee" representing the four houses dominated executive and judicial officials. During recesses a senate, responsible to the estates, in which the king merely had a casting vote, was the executive.

Deep factionalism was manifest when the estates met in 1738. A faction called the "Hats," reacting against the peaceful policy of Chancellor Count Horn over the past 20 years, took control and sought to restore Sweden to great-power

[5]The Swedish events here recounted follow the narrative in the article "Sweden" in the thirteenth edition of the *Encyclopaedia Britannica* (London and New York, 1926). See note 8, below, for some general histories also covering the period.

status. The losing faction was the "Caps," originally called "night-caps" by their opponents. The Hats got into war with Russia, were defeated, and extricated themselves by electing a cousin of the Russian Empress heir to the Swedish throne. He succeeded in 1751 and tried unsuccessfully to seize power in 1756; he was humiliated, but not dethroned. The Hats then lost another war but held a narrow control of the estates by parliamentary maneuver until 1765.

The Caps took over in 1765, shifted to alliance with Russia instead of France, and adopted economic measures of a highly deflationary character. These led to widespread protest movements, the suppression of which the king evidently prevented by refusing to discharge his functions. (The next king was required to promise to "rule continuously.") The Caps had to convene the estates in 1769. In the preliminaries of the session, the French Embassy openly bought the Hats, extracting a promise from them to reform the constitution in a monarchical direction, and the Russian Embassy openly bought the Caps. A Hat marshall of the nobility (head of the estates) was elected and the Cap ministry was dismissed, but the Hats adjourned the estates without restoring monarchical power.

In 1771 the Russian Empress's cousin died and Gustavus III, his son, succeeded. The estates of this year were narrowly divided between Hats and Caps. After long wrangling in 1772, they agreed only to curtail the power of the crown further. At this point, a military coup forced them to reverse themselves and to give the monarch some limited power. A further coup in 1789, which the lower orders supported against the nobility, continued the trend. Real power was now in a military-bureaucratic complex, of which a strong king could manage to be the head. In spite of a regency from 1792 to 1796, the century ended with a monarch on the throne who was something of an autocrat.

French developments in the eighteenth century, like those in Britain in the preceding century, involved a sharpening of conflict to the point where a radical-egalitarian regime succeeded temporarily to power, to be followed by a restored dichotomized regime.[6]

In France the regime clearly showed a two-factional character by the middle of the eighteenth century. Intellectual circles then began generally to espouse an abstract rationalist position which accorded no legitimacy to traditional institutions. The contrary traditionalist view supported the absolute monarchy closely associated with the Catholic Church, adherence to which had been compulsory since 1685. Monarchy and church had become the only functional national institutions. The rationalist position of the left dissolved belief in both.

The absolute monarchy persisted until 1789. Then financial crisis and a lack of effective authority compelled it to reconvene the historical estates for the first time since 1614. The opening to agitation afforded by national elections held in a population wholly without relevant experience completed the dissolution of the authority of the bureaucratic organs of administration dependent upon the monarchy. By the summer of 1789, populistic authorities had taken over the effective powers of government locally, first in Paris and subsequently in most areas of the country. National authority, more moral than coercive, however, continued until the summer of 1792 in a National Assembly of fairly moderate leadership that insisted upon the fiction that the captive king was functioning as a constitutional monarch.

[6]See Crane Brinton, *A Decade of Revolution* (New York, 1938, 1952) for a fuller treatment of the events about to be sketched.

Like England in late 1648, revolutionary France in 1792 suffered extreme frustrations. The aims of the revolutionists had been more simplistic than in the English case, since French dissident leaders had had no experience before 1789 with representative politics nor had they had the alternative experience of elaborating new ecclesiastical forms of belief and organization, so important in the background of the Scots and of the English Puritans. By 1792 it was apparent that the mere denial of the principles of the old order (the abolition of "privileges") could not produce a generally satisfactory new order. Internal disorganization was coupled with foreign invasion. Those who expressed the most extreme egalitarian slogans found themselves able to take over. In Paris mobs could intimidate even the National Assembly. In 1792 they forced the Assembly to dethrone the king and to charge him with criminal acts, an event altogether analogous to Pride's Purge of the English parliament.

There remained in France nothing equivalent to the officer corps of the New Model. The triumph in the "streets" over what vestiges remained of bureaucratically organized authority was clear and unequivocal. Suitable expressions of extreme egalitarian sentiment could activate a "mob," or a "body of patriots," as one may choose to call it, either in Paris or in most other cities. There was no countervailing power. Clearly Criterion 1 (the case of general egalitarian sentiment) and Criterion 3 (the revolutionary case) apply.

The radical-egalitarian regime was more perdurant than in England. With the election of a Convention to replace the National Assembly, almost all known leaders disappeared from view. They were replaced by new men, all, at least ostensibly, highly radical. The only instrumental view of current problems that the highly abstract leftist ideology of France afforded took the form of a conviction that many persons, perhaps a majority of the population, had been hopelessly corrupted by traditional institutions and that therefore the only chance for the now rational institutional arrangements to have their proper benign effect depended upon physically removing from the scene large numbers of corrupt people. (In contrast, the English Puritans had had a deep belief that most men were sinful in any case, and the later Russian Communist revolutionaries possessed an elaborate rationale that prevented them from expecting the millenium to follow the mere removal of older authorities.) The Convention leadership became committed to a policy of terror under which special courts, with a minimum of procedural safeguards and of opportunities for defense, condemned to death persons against whom charges of disloyalty were brought. Only in the speed and efficiency with which the guillotine produced corpses was there hope that the true virtue of republican citizenship might show itself in spite of the corruption imposed by past history on the race.

As obvious adherents of the old order came into short supply, suspicion could only attach to the leaders of the revolution itself. The terror threatened to eat into the ranks of its makers. In one of the great dumb shows of history, the event called Thermidor, an action of obvious but unexpressed meaning, the Convention in the summer of 1794 turned upon its principal leader, Robespierre, and essentially without explanation, sent him to the revolutionary tribunal. The mob rose to defend Robespierre, but by this time there were disciplined troops insensitive to egalitarian slogans. In spite of anything the sloganeers could do, "administration," absent since the summer of 1789, ran its course. Robespierre was executed. No one admitted to even a change of policy, but immediately conservative voices were loudly raised and the radical-egalitarians were obviously without serious power.

Thus, Criteria 1 and 3 cease to apply. In the shock and disillusionment, the rancor and the recrimination, there could be no doubt that the legitimacy of existing institutions was weak. Military intervention in politics was obviously possible. Criterion 5 thus applies. Criterion 7 also again becomes applicable. It may be objected that the extreme radicalism previously dominant must have survived as an important force. Whether or not this was strictly true (and without control of the formal institutions of government, the extreme left lacked any very effective organization), the extreme left was in any case not distinct. The official ruling personnel were essentially the same as during the Terror. Their expressed political position was essentially as before. The radical-egalitarian left was not yet distinct from the generalized left, the socially critical moiety within the dichotomy. A dichotomized regime was thus restored by Thermidor.

A republic, professedly the same regime that dated from the beginning of the Terror in 1792, limped on until 1799. Then a military coup installed Napoleon Bonaparte as the ruler of France. This involved no change in the applicability of the criteria. The regime continued dichotomized.

One further change in the roster of nation-states completes the political history of the eighteenth century from the standpoint of the present study. In 1789 the thirteen former colonies of Great Britain on the coast of North America, which had rebelled and were known as the United States of America, consolidated under a newly erected central government. Thus, a second representative-consensual regime, in addition to that of Britain, came into existence. As colonies, the "states" had been very nearly self-governing. A mature social organization had put forward native leadership impatient of subordinance to what seemed essentially foreign interests. Accomplished technically by the mere separation of the

British colonial governors (who did not even exist in two of the colonies) from control of administration, the rebellion, like that of Parliament in England in 1642, had involved no essential interruption of customary governing processes. The native elite, accustomed to a common stand of resistance to the few British officials, saw itself (in their absence) as essentially united. Even the projected merger of important aspects of power at the national level in the consolidation of 1789 failed to arouse jealousies and rivalries sufficient to block its execution. To most political leaders it was essential to the preservation of independence and it was not seen as threatening seriously their own attained status. Criteria 1, 2, 3, and 4 clearly do not apply. The institutions both of the separate states and of the new national government were clearly defined. Their authority was taken for granted by persons of influence. Therefore Criterion 5 does not apply. There is no basis for the application of Criterion 6.

THE NINETEENTH CENTURY

As has been indicated, there were eight polities that can be considered nation-states in 1800: Denmark, France, Portugal, Russia, Spain, and Sweden had dichotomized regimes; the regimes of Great Britain and the United States were representative-consensual.

Great Britain continued to have a representative-consensual regime throughout the century after altering its name to "The United Kingdom of Great Britain and Ireland" by virtue of the formal absorption in 1801 of the previously dependent but separate Kingdom of Ireland into the basic polity. The United States barely escaped dismemberment through the secession of the Southern states in the Civil War of 1860–1865, but the classification of the regime was not altered. In fact, the seceding area also had a representative-consensual regime. In both the United States and the United Kingdom, representation extended to wider circles within the population as the century advanced. It is possible to regard both as basically "democratic" at the close of the century.

Without formal secession from the British Empire and, indeed, without attaining any recognized international status during the century, two additional polities of British antecedents became distinct and internally autonomous during the period: New Zealand, which had cabinet government after 1856, and Canada, similarly governed after its formation through the federation of previously distinct colonies in 1867. Complete independence for internal purposes is difficult to date in these cases since it was neither demanded nor formally granted. Substantially, on a *de facto* basis, it existed in both countries long before the end of the century. In each case, local elites, which saw themselves as basically unified, had taken over control from the British in much the same way as had happened more dramatically in the American Revolutionary War. Thus, Criteria 5 and 6 as well as Criteria 1, 2, 3, and 4 are inapplicable from as far back as one may judge independence to extend. Therefore, both had representative-consensual regimes.

A further accretion to the number of nation-states with representative-consensual regimes came with the formation of the Kingdom of the Netherlands at the close of the Napoleonic Wars in 1814. The several Dutch provinces had never before been more than loosely united except under the immediately preceding regime imposed by the French. However, the process by which independence from Spain had been secured in the late 1500's and early 1600's had tended to leave the local elites unified and accustomed to institutionalized politics. At least some of the several provinces, which had formed separate polities before the French Revolutionary wars, had probably had representative-consensual regimes. At those times when common action of the provinces seemed necessary, the head of the Orange family had frequently been given the place of command—that of stadholder—which otherwise was in abeyance. Thus, the House of Orange had long been a kind of informal and *de facto* Dutch royal house, a status that was formalized with little difficulty in 1814. At that time there remained little sentiment for reconstituting the provinces as independent polities. The enthronement of the House of Orange, given its previous role, was hardly more than constitutional adjustment. In no sense was a "traditional" monarchy created in 1814. Thus Criterion 4 as well as Criteria 1, 2, and 3 are inapplicable. Except for the initial inclusion of the Belgian area, which lacked the long republican tradition of the Northern low countries and differed in national culture, a stable institutional pattern of constitutional monarchy was established in 1814 with the general consent of the Dutch influential. There is no indication that either Criterion 5 or Criterion 6 applies at any time thereafter to the Netherlands.[7]

Sweden also joined the ranks of polities with representative-consensual regimes shortly after the beginning of the century. The ruling monarch was deeply disliked in upper bureaucratic-military circles and was blamed for serious international reverses, fundamentally the loss of Finland to Russia. In 1809 the military dethroned Gustav IV Adolph and established his uncle, Duke Karl, who was old and childless, as regent. The estates were convened. They ratified the deposition of the monarch and excluded his descendants from the succession. Thus there was no heir to the throne. Within

[7]See Bernard H. M. Vlekke, *Evolution of the Dutch Nation* (New York, 1945).

two weeks, an elaborate constitution, setting up distinct and independent legislative, executive, and judicial authorities, was drafted by a committee and adopted by the estates. The monarch was to be a strong but strictly limited chief executive. The judges were made independent by being exempted from the royal power to remove officials from office. The estates—still quadricameral—held the power over finances as well as the right, jointly with the king, to legislate. The regent was enthroned as Karl XIII, but the problem of finding a new royal family continued. First a prince of Denmark was made heir to the throne, but he died after a year under what were made out to be mysterious circumstances and with the sequel that a prominent courtier, suspected of poisoning him, was lynched on the streets of Stockholm. Eventually, the Prince of Ponte Corvo, born Jean Baptiste Bernadotte, one of Napoleon Bonaparte's field marshalls, was made crown prince. (He reigned eventually as Karl XIV.) After these somewhat disorderly and in appearance accidental events, Swedish institutions became firmly fixed for the first time. There occur no further irregular seizures of power. The strained partisanship of the eighteenth century did not reappear. Criteria 1, 2, and 3 are inapplicable. With the Bernadottes on the throne (after 1818) there is clearly no traditional monarchy. Criterion 4 is thus inapplicable. There are no grounds after 1809 for applying Criteria 5 or 6.

Just how the Swedish stabilization was accomplished in 1809 is unclear from the historical record.[8] Influence at that time was largely confined to upper military-bureaucratic

[8]See Ragnar Svanström and Carl Fredrik Palmstierna, *A Short History of Sweden,* trans. Joan Bulman (Oxford, 1934), pp. 315–324; Carl Hallendorf and Adolf Schuck, *History of Sweden,* trans. Lajla Yapp (Stockholm, 1929), pp. 360–364; Ingvar Andersson, *A History of Sweden,* trans. Carolyn Hannay (London, 1956), pp. 304–316.

circles, whose members kept their counsel very tightly and seem to have left no very revealing memoirs. It seems probable that behind the scenes in the deliberations of the constitutional committee and in the intrigues by which an heir to the throne was eventually secured, the essential abstract features of the British settlement of 1689 must have been reproduced, that is, all interests that were to remain influential in the immediate future were satisfactorily accommodated to each other and assured of security against each other within the system. While the repudiation of principles, which in the British case guaranteed against the sense of righteousness necessary to reopen past factional struggles on an unlimited basis, is less conspicuous in the Swedish case (perhaps necessarily so because the quarter century of bureaucratic-military dictatorship had suppressed the overt badges and labels of the previous factionalism), still a trace of the renunciation of causes can be found. To establish a strong, even if constitutional, monarch could not have set well with the extreme liberal sentiment which had appealed strongly to the peasantry in the eighteenth century, yet it was historically far more acceptable to peasants than to nobles, since strong monarchs in the Swedish tradition were associated with attacks on the status of the aristocrats. The Swedish nobility was no more monarchist than the Polish had been.

A further addition during the century to the ranks of nation-states having representative-consensual regimes was Switzerland.[9] In 1848, after a civil war among the cantons, a federation like that of the United States was established. The cantons were brought together under a strong central government. As in the case of the Netherlands, except during the period of dominance by the French Revolutionary armies,

[9]See Robert C. Brooks, *Government and Politics of Switzerland* (Yonkers-on-Hudson, N.Y., 1918).

the Swiss cantons, although normally linked in a loose confederation, had never before constituted a single polity under central institutions with real governing power. This institutional pattern proved highly stable. Clearly, none of the criteria apply to the regime established under the constitution of 1848. Presumably, the arrangements involved in the federal constitution offered an assurance of protection to all important interests that continued to be influential after the union.

Conditions under which national independence was attained seem in two other cases, Belgium and Norway, to have fallen just short of what might have been necessary for establishing representative-consensual regimes.

Belgium is historically merely the southern portion of the so-called "low countries," which also include the modern Netherlands. The whole area had had a common history down to the war for independence from Spain in the late sixteenth century. The northern provinces, now called the Netherlands, succeeded in establishing and maintaining their independence at this time. As a result, Protestantism in this area remained dominant for a long period. The southern provinces, however, shortly fell back under Spanish rule and came again to be Catholic in religion. They remained under foreign rule until the defeat of Napoleon in 1814. They were then assigned by the powers to the new Kingdom of the Netherlands, but after two centuries of separation this also amounted to foreign rule. The Belgians successfully rebelled in 1830. They set up a representative system of government and chose a king from a German princely family. Clearly Criteria 1, 2, 3, and 4 do not apply to his regime. Moreover, governmental institutions (except for two periods of German military occupation) have been stable until the present day. The military coup has been no part of the normal political repertory. Criterion 5 thus does not apply. There have been deeply felt ideological divisions, however, whch have made it exceedingly difficult for factions out of power to accept as morally legitimate the policies decided upon by their opponents. Catholics and Liberals were deeply divided during the nineteenth century over the question of religious as against secular schooling. Thus Criterion 6 applies. The regime is trichotomized without a right.[10]

Norway came into modern times as a dependency of Denmark. With the sanction of the victorious powers after the Napoleonic wars, Sweden undertook to absorb Norway by force as compensation for her loss of Finland to Russia. Meanwhile, the Norwegians had declared their independence, adopted a constitution providing for representative government, and elected their last Danish governor as king. The Swedes prevailed, but only after accepting the established Norwegian constitution. The Swedish king became the ruler of Norway under the Norwegian constitution, but Sweden acquired the right to represent Norway for international purposes. Representatives of the Swedish government directed and supervised the executive government in Norway and attempted to guide the legislature until 1884 when a Norwegian cabinet responsible to the Norwegian legislature was conceded. It is from this point that Norway may be regarded as *de facto* an independent polity in internal matters. As in the case of Belgium, the institutions thus established have been stable (except for one period of German occupation). Thus, the first five criteria are inapplicable. As in Belgium, however, there appears to have been a deeply felt ideological

[10]See Thomas Harrison Reed, *Government and Politics of Belgium* (Yonkers-on-Hudson, N.Y., 1924).

division, and Criterion 6 applies.[11] Throughout the last half of the nineteenth century there was a sharp division between Conservatives and Liberals, though the struggle for independence from Swedish control seems to have muted this difference from the 1880's to 1905, and the seeking of national independence, which no faction opposed, is normally stressed in brief histories of the period.

Five other European nation-states came into existence during the nineteenth century, all with main-stem regimes with a right: Greece (1830), Romania (1878), Serbia (1878), Germany (1870), Italy (1870). Japan acquired the general characteristics of a nation-state of Western type before the end of the century, also with a main-stem regime with a right. Criteria 1, 2, and 3 are inapplicable in these cases (except that Criterion 3 may have applied in Japan before the full centralization of administration in the 1880's). Criterion 4 applies in all cases except that of Italy, since a real monarch in each of the other cases could, with more or less plausibility, act as one who owned his office and who appeared in general to

[11]There was a deep cultural division in nineteenth-century Norway (reflected in the language controversy of recent times) between the Danish-speaking "official class," dominant in the cities, and the peasantry (mostly landowning), who spoke local dialects. In the middle of the century, peasants were beginning to elect representatives from their own class to the Storting. The bureaucrats, as the dominant interest of the country, for a time became adherents of the Swedish monarchy as a means of holding the rising "democracy" in check. Eventually a strong Liberal party formed around peasant interests. Later, the Conservatives found it necessary to organize as a party. See Hjalmar H. Boyesen, *The Story of Norway* (New York, 1894), especially p. 528. Karen Larsen speaks of "the vituperative bitterness of the factional and personal strife" around 1889 and says that the "feelings" of the peasantry "against the upper class were expressed with a bitter boldness," in *A History of Norway* (Princeton, 1948), p. 459. See also G. Gathorne Hardy, *Norway* (New York, 1925) and Knut Gjerset, *History of the Norwegian People* (New York, 1932).

control the military and the bureaucracy. In Italy there was sufficient social unrest and lack of institutional prestige in governing institutions so that Criterion 5 applies. Through the end of the nineteenth century, Criterion 7 is also applicable in all cases except those of Germany and Italy. The other regimes are therefore dichotomized. For Germany and Italy, Criterion 7 does not apply, and the regimes are trichotomized with a right from their origins. In Italy, although (because of suffrage restrictions) the Socialists did not acquire significant parliamentary representation until 1913, radical-egalitarians were recognized as an important political force in the later nineteenth century, and the generalized left had become clearly differentiated from them as a movement of men of property.[12] In Germany a Catholic Center, mingling traditional religious appeals with some degree of practical "welfare-state-ism," was an important force from almost the beginning of the Empire.[13]

Of the five nation-states other than Sweden with dichotomized regimes at the beginning of the century, Russia, Spain, and Portugal still had this type of regime at the end. In Russia the reliance on bureaucratic institutions continued without serious alteration. Before 1900 there was no sufficiently large and differentiated body of radical-egalitarians to make Criterion 7 inapplicable. Shortly thereafter, in the cases of Spain and Portugal it is necessary to recognize such forces as distinct from the traditional generalized left, but in 1900 these regimes were probably still dichotomized.

[12]See Henry Russell Spencer, *Government and Politics of Italy* (Yonkers-on-Hudson, N.Y., 1932).

[13]The German Reich (or "Empire") was formed in 1870 by a federal constitution acceded to by the various German states other than Austria, most of them more or less traditional monarchies. See Fritz-Konrad Kruger, *Government and Politics of the German Empire* (Yonkers-on-Hudson, N.Y., 1915).

For Denmark Criterion 7 ceases to be applicable and the regime changes from dichotomized to trichotomized with a right before the end of the century. The change probably occurred by 1880. In 1870 farmers formed the so-called "Left" party, but shortly thereafter the first violent clashes over incipient working-class organization in the towns occurred. There was soon a potentially powerful radical-egalitarian left although the Socialists did not attain 10 per cent of the seats in the popular house until 1898. This left the farmers' party basically a propertied movement.[14]

For France also Criterion 7 becomes inapplicable before the end of the century, though the highly developed "leftist" ideology of the exceedingly numerous and politically influential petty bourgeoisie in that country superficially preserved a political rhetoric appropriate to the generalized left of a dichotomized regime. This large portion of the population reacted readily against the aristocrat, the priest, the rich man, or even the man of prominence of any sort. "As the twentieth century approached, however, the petty bourgeoisie and the wealthier peasant discovered that there was a radicalism more radical than their own."[15] They liked to identify with the radicals of 1792 but not with those of 1870, and though in many cases they called themselves "radical socialists," they had no real affinity to the growing movement styled "socialist," pure and simple.

France and Spain in the nineteenth century exemplify a kind of highly conspicuous instability of regimes which often advertises the fundamental lack of legitimacy of main-stem regimes with a right.

Nineteenth-century France consisted culturally of two dis-

[14] John Danstrop, *A History of Denmark* (2d ed.; Copenhagen, 1949) especially pp. 124–125.

[15] John B. Wolf, *France: 1815 to the Present* (New York, 1940), p. 431

tinct nations. The "right" was monarchical and Catholic. The "left" was "republican" and anticlerical, if not openly agnostic. Thus, the dichotomy presumed in the stereotype characteristic of dichotomized regimes was in France very much a matter of fact. The higher bureaucracy was always infiltrated by the right, and the upper levels of wealth and family status were largely rightist. A large part of the population, however—outside certain traditionalist and relatively religious areas—tended to respond to the ideological appeals of leftist political leaders. All political contests tended to be seen as a re-enactment of the Great Revolution, which the left glorified and the right deprecated.

In this atmosphere no regime had much legitimacy except to its partisans. The "revolutionary" republic was replaced in 1799 by a military dictatorship in which a general of the revolutionary armies, Napoleon Bonaparte, made himself emperor. Displaced by foreign intervention in 1815, this regime was succeeded by a restoration of the legitimate monarchy, accompanied now by parliamentary institutions resting on a highly limited suffrage. A popular uprising in 1830 changed the person of the monarch without altering the structure of the regime. In 1848 popular uprisings in Paris of highly radical motivation set up a Second Republic but, in contrast with 1789, no disintegration of bureaucratic authority took place in the provinces. The Second Republic passed into the control of moderate leadership as the result of elections, and then, after the heir of the first emperor had been elected president, was transformed into a monarchical regime, the Second Empire. This regime was terminated by a military disaster in 1870 (defeat by Germany), which was followed by a repetition of the events of 1848—the setting up of a Third Republic by radical forces in Paris and the substitution of moderate leadership by popular elections. The Third Republic was allowed to continue as such only because the various monarchical factions (legitimist, Imperial, and Orleanist) in its first parliament could not agree on which king to restore. Moderate "leftist" forces, however, soon came to dominate elections, and the Third Republic persisted until the German invasion of 1940.

None of these regimes, as has been said, had much legitimacy. Only during the Restoration, from 1815 to 1830, was the regime strictly acceptable to extreme rightist sentiment, though the ambiguous imperial regimes and the Orleanist monarchy of 1830 obviously appealed to less strict conservatives. The three republics were weakly supported in highly influential circles. The long duration of the Third Republic may perhaps be explained in part by the fact that obstensible power lay with leaders conspicuous in representative politics but unable (and unwilling in principle) to provide a strong executive, while much of the practical administration of the state was in the hands of rightists strategically placed in the upper bureaucracy. As to the applicability of the criteria, Criterion 4 applies from 1814 to 1830, Criterion 5 applies during the rest of the century, and Criterion 7 applies up to some time between 1870 and 1900.

Objective manifestations of the right-left dichotomy came suddenly in Spain in the convulsions following the kidnapping of the royal family by the French Emperor Napoleon I and his imposition of his brother Joseph as King of Spain in 1808.[16] (Spain was at the time heavily garrisoned with French troops, who had come as allies.) The suddenness of the appearance of clashing ideological principles is perhaps ascribable to the fact that the development of resistance to

[16]Geoffrey de Grandmaison, *L'Espagne et Napoleon, 1804–1809* (Paris 1908).

the French threw much greater influence to certain urban areas, particularly the Seville region. The kidnapping of the royal family had the effect of breaking the continuity of traditional political institutions once and for all, since the subsequent history of the restored monarchy after 1814 did not present a picture around which traditionalistic attitudes could readily be rebuilt. Of traditional institutions only the Church maintained continuity. Thus, the Church more than the monarchy was the later rallying point of the right.

While the monarch was forcibly detained in France, resistance forces necessarily had to resort to more or less representative juntas as a way of legitimizing the various military mutinies which, with popular support, immediately challenged the French occupying forces. Control of the resistance, as it spread, moreover, fell largely to an elected parliament located at Cadiz and dominated by "Liberals." Thus, in the few years of the French intervention, much of Spain had the experience of the rapid substitution (at least nominally) of "rational" for "traditional" institutions and principles. As in France during the early stages of the Revolution, this experience left a large potential support for the later "right" in the form of outraged religious opinion.

From 1814 to 1877 a Liberal and a Conservative faction battled—fairly literally—for control of the state.[17] The battles occurred concurrently in the parliamentary arena and in that of the politics of the military coup and the *pronunciamiento,* with all changes of partisan control in fact determined by military rather than by electoral events.

In 1814 the returning monarch, Ferdinand VII, ignored the Cadiz authorities (who sought to welcome him as a constitu-

[17]See H. Butler Clarke, *Modern Spain 1815–1898* (Cambridge, 1906), and A. Ramos Oliveira, *Politics, Economics and Men of Modern Spain* (London, 1946).

tional monarch) and established an absolute monarchy. Briefly from 1820 to 1823, however, Liberal military officers dominated the state and held Ferdinand a prisoner. French intervention in 1823 restored Ferdinand's absolutist regime. An extreme traditionalistic movement was then given formal organization, supported to a large extent by ecclesiastical personnel, and led by the heir apparent, Don Carlos. Ferdinand, however, on his deathbed in 1833, took action to reopen the succession to females. The refusal of the extreme traditionalists to recognize this action underlay the endemic "Carlist" revolt in the northern provinces throughout much of the rest of the century.

Ferdinand's daughter Isabel (a girl of three in 1833) nominally reigned as Queen of Spain from 1833 until 1868. In view of the traditionalist defection under Don Carlos, her government had to be given parliamentary form promptly as a means of securing Liberal support. Ostensibly, the Spanish governmental system was parliamentary with responsible cabinets during the remainder of Isabel's reign, but, as has been said, military interventions actually determined the changes of partisan control. The regime was Liberal from 1835 to 1843 and from 1854 to 1856, otherwise Conservative.

In 1868 Liberals were still prominent in the officer corps, as they had been since the period of resistance to the French. Finding Isabel's court more largely infiltrated than usual by adherents of the Carlist faction, Liberal officers overthrew the dynasty in that year. After a brief interlude with a hired Italian monarch (who resigned), the administration disintegrated under a weak Republic, extremist social-leveling movements sweeping widely over the countryside. The military restored a son of Isabel to the throne in 1877, and Spain thereafter experienced the novelty of a stable regime without open military intervention until after World War I. This

Restoration regime was almost wholly dominated by the landowning class but, like Isabel's government, it was parliamentary in form. A tame Conservative and a tame Liberal party alternated in power at arranged intervals, elections being rigged through a system of recognized local political bosses. No change in the applicability of the criteria accompanied these changes of regime except the alternate applicability of Criterion 4, which applies until 1808, from 1814 to 1820, from 1823 to 1833, and after 1877, and Criterion 5 which applies during the rest of the century; Criterion 7 is applicable throughout the century.

No attempt will be made to deal with the nation-states of Latin America individually in this period. Of the twenty states now in this category, all except Cuba and Panama could be considered nation-states in 1900. None of Criteria 1, 2, and 4 apply to the eighteen Latin American republics of the time. Criterion 5, however, applies in all cases. Most had a well-established pattern of military politics as the only real method of changing administrations and, while constitutional oligarchical regimes had been fairly stable in the late nineteenth century in Argentina and Chile, there was widespread dissent from the legitimacy of these regimes on the part of interests excluded from effective representation. Criterion 3 applies to Haiti and possibly in some other cases. Criterion 7 seems applicable to most, if not all, the other polities. Thus, most Latin American regimes were dichotomized in 1900, and those that were not were traditional or (possibly) trichotomized with a right.

The experience of political instability in Spain in the nineteenth century had been practically reduplicated in the various Latin American countries. These were mostly carved out of the Spanish Empire as the immediate or the delayed result of the lapse of traditional authority in Spain during the

French intervention from 1808 to 1814, although Brazil was governed until 1889 by a hereditary monarch of the Portuguese line. Nowhere had there been experience with representative government before independence, and no clear national areas were then recognized. Politics initially depended almost wholly on military force. In most cases, the political struggle appeared as a two-way contest between Liberal and Conservative factions, usually so-called as in Spain, during some period in the nineteenth century. As in Spain, regimes were ostensibly representative, but the allegiance of the military forces to different personalities actually determined the installation and deposition of successive administrations. The Conservatives, as in Spain, were closely associated with the Church and with a native aristocratic landed class. The Liberals tended to represent less traditional wealth and were in various degrees anticlerical. In a few countries, a traditional aristocratic class was initially weak or soon lost its dominant position. In these cases most politicians tended to profess to be Liberal, but, as in the other cases, political power was transmitted by events of strictly military rather than electoral politics, and military dictators (who might call themselves Liberal) functioned as a *de facto* right. Although a few personal dictatorships were very long lasting, few countries maintained even an ostensible constitutional succession to office for any lengthy period. Argentina and Chile, however, with stable oligarchic representative regimes were exceptions. A similar but briefer stabilization of constitutional forms occurred in Colombia in the 1920's. Stability in these cases evidently depended on the ability of the Conservatives to dominate elections. After this condition did not hold (Argentina 1916, Chile 1920, Colombia 1930), there was a more or less rapid reversion to open military participation in politics (Argentina 1930, Chile 1924, Colombia 1949).

As was indicated in Chapter I, the theory to be later advanced will associate types of regimes in certain ways with socioeconomic levels. Representative-consensual regimes do not occur at Level 1. Dichotomized regimes are associated with Level 2, but trichotomized regimes with or without a right do not occur at Levels 1 and 2. Thus, the history of regimes so far recorded (Latin America being ignored), if the theory is valid, indicates that none of the nation-states in the period discussed were at Level 1, that all of them except perhaps those with representative-consensual regimes were at Level 2 during the seventeenth and eighteenth centuries, and that the polities with main-stem regimes were still at that level at or about 1900 with the exceptions of Belgium, Germany, Italy, and Norway, which were above Level 2 from their respective origins in 1830, 1870, 1870, and 1884, and Denmark and France, which rose from Level 2 to Level 3 late in the century.

Such data as exist are compatible with these requirements for the validity of the theory. The time-series set out in Chapter II show that Germany, Italy, and Norway were at Level 3 in the late nineteenth century. A similar time-series could be constructed from similar data for Belgium, except that, because 16 is not a plausible value for *ac* in this case, the values for earlier years would be uncertain.[18] Nevertheless, any plausible guess for *ac* from 16 to 30 in the several census years shows the country clearly within Level 3 in 1880 (the first year for which data are available) and thereafter. For Denmark the time-series in Chapter II shows Level 3 clearly from 1901. The case of France is similar to that of Belgium. Even though by 1962 the value of *ac* was only 18, the very

[18]Data for 1880, 1890, 1910, 1920, and 1930 in Colin Clark, *The Conditions of Economic Progress* (London, 1940), p. 203. Our Table 2 above shows the value of *ac* to be 27 in 1947.

large number of tiny commercial establishments continually reported by observers indicates that in earlier years this value was very high. Assuming *ac* = 20 gives a *da* of 38, well into Level 3, by 1906 and, even if *ac* is assumed to be 30, the resulting *da* of 28 is high in the transitional interval between Level 2 and Level 3.[19] Five of the seven countries with representative-consensual regimes at the end of the century—Canada, the Netherlands, Sweden, Switzerland, and the United States—were also at Level 3.[20] The United Kingdom, as indicated in Chapter II, was already in the transitional range from Level 3 to Level 4. New Zealand may possibly have also reached this transitional range.[21] For other nation-states covered in the narrative, evidence indicating level in 1899 (independently of the theoretical requirement) is largely lacking. Japan, as indicated in Chapter II, was just entering the transitional range between Levels 2 and 3. Russia seems to have been fairly low in the *da* range normally indicating Level 2.[22]

[19]Values of *ag* of 42 for both 1906 and 1921 are given in Table 4, League of Nations, *International Statistical Yearbook 1929* (Geneva, 1930). Values of 37, 36, and 27 for *ag* in 1936, 1946, and 1954 respectively are given in Table 12, 1948 number, Table 13, 1949–50 number, and Table 12, 1956 number, *Demographic Yearbook*. Table 13, 1964 number, allows computation of *ac* 18 for 1962.

[20]This is indicated by the time-series in Chapter II except for the Netherlands. Data in Clark, *op. cit.,* p. 203, support estimates by the usual procedures indicating Level 3 for the Netherlands in 1899.

[21]Estimates by the usual procedures from data in Table 4, *International Statistical Yearbook 1929,* gives a *da* of 58 for New Zealand in 1911, indicating the range between Levels 3 and 4.

[22]George A. Vernadsky, *A History of Russia* (New Haven, 1951), p. 198, gives 74 per cent as the proportion of the population dependent on agriculture in 1897. If this figure is treated as *ag, da* estimated by the usual procedure is 10.

THE TWENTIETH CENTURY THROUGH 1965

This period begins with seven nation-states having representative-consensual regimes (Canada, the Netherlands, New Zealand, Sweden, Switzerland, the United Kingdom, the United States) and ends with twelve. The additions are Australia, Denmark, Ireland, Mexico, and Norway. In two, possibly four, of these cases the representative-consensual character of the regime dates from the establishment or the re-establishment as an independent polity of the nation-state in which it occurs. The Commonwealth of Australia came into existence in 1901 through the federation under British authority of several distinct Australian colonies. For internal purposes it was substantially independent from this time. None of the criteria subsequently applies. By insurrection Ireland (exclusive of the northeastern counties) secured from the British government in 1921 recognition of internal independence analogous to that possessed by Canada at the time. None of the criteria applies thereafter. The liberation from Nazi occupation in 1945 may be the first occasion on which none of the criteria applies in the cases of both Denmark and Norway, though there is some possibility that a closer acquaintance with their histories than is possessed by the present writer would allow predating of the regime classification as representative-consensual to an earlier period.[23]

It will be recalled that the Norwegian regime at the end

[23]That the blurring of ideological distinctions between party positions is now taking place in the Scandinavian countries other than Finland and Iceland seems to be taken for granted by those who write on their politics. Henry Valen and Daniel Katz, *Political Parties in Norway: A Community Study* (Oslo, 1964), p. 33, and Stein Rokkan and Henry Valen, "Parties, Elections, and Political Behavior in the Northern Countries: A Review of Recent Research," *Politische Forschungen*, I (1960), 103–136.

of the nineteenth century was classified as trichotomized without a right. This classification clearly holds until well into the 1930's, if not until the Nazi occupation in 1940. By essentially unilateral action on the part of Norway, the connection with Sweden was broken in 1905 and a distinct monarchical line installed. Shortly thereafter, highly radical-egalitarian tendencies grew to dominance in the Labor or Socialist party, which already had some parliamentary representation. In 1918 this party, by then rather large, joined the Third International. Moderate elements split off as the Social Democrats in 1921. The radical leaders withdrew the party from the International in 1923. In 1927 they had returned to a sufficiently moderate position so that the seceding group felt able to return. By 1935 the party's position had so moderated that, although it lacked a majority of its own, it succeeded in forming a cabinet and was still in office at the time of the German invasion in 1940. After the liberation in 1945 the Labor party won a clear majority. All this suggests a steady diminution of Socialist ideological distinctness, and hence of ideological division in general, after the high point in the early twenties. Thus, a closer appraisal of these events may lead to the conclusion that Criterion 6 ceases to apply at some time before the German occupation.

Criterion 4 alone applies to Denmark at the end of the nineteenth century, indicating that the regime was trichotomized with a right, the right being embodied in the monarchical institutions. In 1901, however, cabinet responsibility to the legislature was conceded, ending the applicability of Criterion 4. If no other criterion then becomes applicable, it would be necessary to classify the regime as representative-consensual from 1901. Since no trace of military intervention in politics occurs in the subsequent period, Criterion 5 does not become applicable. It appears to the present writer that the positions taken over the next three decades by the several parties, particularly by the peasant "Left" (the real conservatives at the time) as over against the Social Democrats, indicate a fairly acute ideological division such that Criterion 6 probably applies from 1901. Thus, the regime then became trichotomized without a right. As with Norway, there is a question as to whether Criterion 6 continues applicable until the German occupation in 1940. In Denmark there was a significant political compromise in 1933 in which the Social Democrats and the "Left" joined in making possible legislation of marked interest to each of their followings separately, farm legislation being in effect exchanged for a substantial revision of the body of social legislation. This was a sharp enough departure from the then normal political alignment so that it may mark the point at which Criterion 6 ceases to apply and the regime becomes representative-consensual.[24]

The fifth addition to the ranks of representative-consensual regimes in the twentieth century definitely did not coincide with the establishment or re-establishment of the polity in which it occurred. Like the earlier changes in England in 1689 and in Sweden in 1809, it occurred in a continuing polity by the transformation of a previously dichotomized regime. This is the case of Mexico and the date of the transformation appears to have been 1933. Mexico's political history in the nineteenth century was similar to that of other Latin American countries in that political power ultimately depended upon personal control of military forces. Criteria 5 and 7 are applicable. Any strictly traditional and aristocratic upper class—the "traditionalist-personalist right" in

[24]See John Danstrop, *op. cit.*, especially pp. 156–157 for the agreement of 1933. See also J. S. Birch, *Denmark in History* (London, 1938), especially p. 406 with respect to the type of political postures on the basis of which we incline to believe that Criterion 6 applies after 1901.

the sense of the stereotype characteristic of dichotomized regimes—had been undermined in successive struggles.[25] The century ended under the long Diaz dictatorship, a conservative regime though not in the traditional sense. The so-called Mexican Revolution began in 1910. By the middle 1920's it had created a largely new elite, mostly generals, largely of the "institutionalist-personalist left" in terms of the dichotomized stereotype. Criterion 5 still applies. The end of a presidential term was expected to produce a civil war through which a successor would be selected. Criterion 7 also applies. There was, as yet, no important radical-egalitarian left seen as distinct from the general body of the socially critical. In 1928 the president and dominant general, Calles, facing an awkward situation created by the assassination of the president-elect, was able to persuade the military to stand aside for the moment and then undertook to organize for the first time a plausible structure for the ruling party of the "Revolution." This structure was perfected over the immediately ensuing years until it seems to have provided a secure channel of representation for all important interests. In 1933 its convention chose Cardenas for president and after his formal election he successfully turned against Calles, who had been generally regarded as the national political boss. Sometime after 1928 Criterion 5 ceases to apply. The 1933 convention of the ruling party seems the most likely occasion. There seems to be no sufficient ground for regarding any other criterion as applicable thereafter. Thus, by a "settlement," abstractly similar to that in England in 1689 and in Sweden in 1809, a representative-consensual regime seems to have been created in Mexico.[26]

[25]See "Mexico" in *Encyclopaedia Britannica* (Chicago, 1957).

[26]For structural aspects of the settlement, particularly the institutional history of the Partido Nacional Revolucionario (PNR), later the Partido

For eight of the twelve nation-states having representative-consensual regimes at the end of 1965, the time-series diagrammed in Chapter II show attained levels in the twentieth century as follows:

Australia	—	Transitional Level 3 to 4 to 1960, then Level 4;
Canada	—	Level 3 to 1931, transitional Level 3 to 4 to 1952, then Level 4;
Denmark	—	Level 3 to 1935, then transitional Level 3 to 4;
Norway	—	Level 3 to 1935, transitional Level 3 to 4 to 1955, then Level 4;
Sweden	—	Level 3 to 1948, transitional Level 3 to 4 to 1955, then Level 4;
Switzerland	—	Level 3 to 1950, then transitional Level 3 to 4;
United Kingdom	—	Transitional Level 3 to 4 to 1925, then Level 4;
United States	—	Level 3 to 1920, transitional Level 3 to 4 to 1935, then Level 4.

In the other four cases, data as to level attained are also available. Data for 1936 and 1951 for Ireland indicate Level 3, for 1961 the transitional range from Level 3 to Level 4, with the end of Level 3 about 1955.[27] Data for 1950 for Mexico indicate the transitional range from Level 2 to Level 3.

Revolucionario Institucional (PRI) see Robert E. Scott, *The Mexican Government in Transition* (Urbana, Ill., 1959). Much light on who did what in the course of the events we interpret as a "settlement" from 1928 to 1933 will be found in John W. F. Dulles, *Yesterday in Mexico: A Chronicle of the Revolution 1919–1936* (Austin, Tex., 1951).

[27]For each year *da* was computed by the preferred method and for 1961 nonmanual *da* was similarly computed. Table 12, 1948 number, Table 16, 1955 number, Table 13, 1964 number, *Demographic Yearbook* for successive years respectively.

Those for 1960 indicate Level 3 with the beginning of Level 3 about 1955.[28] Data for New Zealand indicate the transitional range from Level 3 to Level 4 in 1911, 1921, 1936, and 1951 and Level 4 in 1961, with the beginning of Level 4 about 1957.[29]

In 1900 (aside from any possibilities among the Latin American countries) there were two trichotomized regimes without a right (Norway and Belgium). In 1965 there were seven such regimes. Belgium continued in the category, as the monumental rioting of January 1961 makes clear. Norway, as has been said, acquired a representative-consensual regime. The six additions were Japan, Uruguay, Costa Rica, Iceland, Finland, and Austria.

Criteria 4 and 7 apply to the regime in Japan in 1900. Really influential circles were those that could manipulate the authority of the monarchy. Imported Western political ideas, particularly those of a generalized and not too sweeping liberal variety, were conspicuous in early ventures in partisan organization. As yet, the authoritarian or "traditionalist-personalist" orientation was mainly associated with the court and with the upper bureaucracy rather than with the elective politicians. There was no indication of an important radical-egalitarian trend distinct from the generalized liberal posi-

[28]For each year *da* was computed by the preferred method. For 1960 nonmanual *da* was estimated by the usual procedure. Table 16, 1955 number, and Table 12, 1964 number, *ibid.* for successive years respectively.

[29]*Da* estimated by the usual procedure for 1911 and 1921; computed by preferred method for 1936, 1951, and 1961, as was nonmanual *da* for 1961. Data for 1911 and 1921, Table 4, *International Statistical Yearbook 1929* (Geneva, 1930); for 1936, 1951, and 1961, Table 12, 1948 number, Table 6, 1955 number, Table 13, 1964 number, *Demographic Yearbook,* respectively.

tion.[30] World War I may be taken as the approximate time when Criterion 7 ceases to be applicable. Positions taken by the leading parties had become centrist in the sense that they mingled traditional with somewhat liberal approaches. By this time also it must be assumed that a potentially powerful radical-egalitarian force was recognized as existing, since much governmental policy was thereafter directed successfully to preventing its actualization in strong organization. The trichotomized regime with a right, so formed, was ended by conquest in 1945. When an independent Japanese regime was restored by the peace treaty in 1952, the monarchical court was no longer a center of serious political authority and the formerly prestigious military institutions had been disbanded. Hence neither Criterion 4 nor Criterion 5 applies to the post-War Japanese regime. Criterion 6, however, is applicable and the regime is therefore trichotomized without a right. Even though there is no effective center of authority except the representative governmental structure, extreme differences in ideological traditions between the minority, the Socialists (descended from the perpetually suppressed left of the old regime), and the majority, the Liberal Democrats (descended from the centrist major parties of the old regime), prevent the ready acceptance of governmental decisions. Extreme public disturbances have occurred on several occasions.[31]

Uruguay, like the other Latin American states, had a political history in the nineteenth century in which military politics and civil warfare were the normal avenues of political action. A deeply rooted bifactionalism became traditional, as

[30]Harold S. Quigley, *Japanese Government and Politics* (New York, 1932).

[31]Ardath W. Burks, *The Government of Japan* (2d ed.; New York, 1964).

in Colombia, and even today the important political trends are internal factions of the traditional Colorado and Blanco parties. The first of these was liberal in the generalized sense characteristic of dichotomized regimes and was associated with the metropolis. The second was a conservative faction associated with the rural areas. Clearly Criterion 5 applies at the beginning of the twentieth century. Whether Criterion 7 applies is unclear in sources available to the present writer. The rather sophisticated program of social legislation characteristic of Uruguay from a very early date in the present century suggests that centrist as well as radical-egalitarian forces were probably clearly distinguishable by 1900 or shortly thereafter.

The subsequent stabilization of institutions in Uruguay is commonly attributed to the personal leadership of José Batlle y Ordoñez, who served as president from 1903 to 1907 and again from 1911 to 1915. The last serious uprising against constituted authority, an unsuccessful one, occurred in 1903. Subsequently there have been no *coups d'état* carried out by military factions. Although two presidents took action that was patently unconstitutional, one in 1933 and one in 1942, these actions seem to have been fairly widely accepted as necessary steps to break out of institutional deadlocks, and they did not result in any general reversion to personalized rather than institutionalized politics. It is clear that Criterion 5 has not been applicable since the first term of President Batlle. Thus, the subsequent regime must have been either representative-consensual or trichotomized without a right. The persistence of the traditional bifactional political division and an impression that political positions have frequently been urged with extreme intransigency leads the present writer to the conclusion that Criterion 6 applies and that the regime has been trichotomized without a right.[32]

Next to Uruguay, the Latin American country with the most stable governmental system in the present century has been Costa Rica. Regular successions to office after elections were the rule. However, a general who had seized power was dictator from 1917 to 1919. Criterion 5 is thus applicable. Criterion 7 probably applies until about 1929, in which year a Communist party was organized. Radical-egalitarian forces must have been seen as distinct from the old generalized left from the early 1930's. The regime was thus trichotomized with a right. In 1948 the administration in office, which had flirted with the Communists, refused to accept the results of a presidential election. A rebel force was organized from the civilian population. The army showed little taste for defending the government. Eventually the rebels prevailed. A junta ruled for some months in 1948 and 1949. It dissolved the previous army and its own army, retaining only a police force. The candidate whose election had been annulled was installed in office in 1949. Several subsequent elections have occurred and those elected have served their terms. It seems clear that the social-political changes in 1948 and 1949 were sufficient so that Criterion 5 ceases to apply. The subsequent regime must therefore be either representative-consensual or trichotomized without a right. It seems probable that Criterion 6 applies and that the regime is trichotomized without a right. Although the forces that won the civil war in 1948 have subsequently remained dominant, it appears unlikely that the ideological factionalism then evident has been re-

[32]See Philip B. Taylor, Jr., "Interests and Institutional Dysfunction in Uruguay," *American Political Science Review,* LVII (1963), 62–74.

duced to the degree that would make Criterion 6 inapplicable.[33]

Iceland, after a long history of subordination to Denmark, was recognized as independent for internal purposes in 1918. It was subjected to Allied occupation from 1940 to 1947. Meanwhile, in 1944 it severed all connection with Denmark. Criteria 1, 2, 3, 4, and 5 clearly do not apply after 1947. Because Communists have been of some importance in recent politics and because the Socialists, prominent since the late 1920's, are set off rather sharply from other political forces, there is a degree of ideological tension such that Criterion 6 presumably applies, making the regime trichotomized without a right.

Finland, after having been transferred from the rule of Sweden to that of Russia early in the nineteenth century, continued to be governed by Russia under a regime that allowed some institutional and legal autonomy until the Russian Revolution in 1917. At that time, the Finnish Parliament declared the country's independence. There was no local aristocracy and no local prestigious military institutions. There was a well-established parliament. Representative government was practically inevitable. Components of the Russian Army under radical leadership, however, were still stationed in the country, and political opinion had been deeply divided for about a decade between a set of "bourgeois" parties and a large but minority Social Democratic party. Circumstances led the latter into insurrection. There was a brief civil war in 1918 which the conservative government, aided by German intervention, won. The Social Democrats

[33]Harry Kantor, *The Costa Rican Election of 1953: A Case Study* (Gainesville, Fla., 1958); Franklin D. Parker, *The Central American Republics* (London, 1964); and John D. Martz, *Central America: The Crisis and the Challenge* (Chapel Hill, N.C., 1959).

were not suppressed but they became thereafter a consistently nonrevolutionary movement from which the Communists separated to form what has subsequently been a rather important political tendency. Although the only prominent officer of Finnish extraction in the old Russian Army played a large political role and long served as president, the military never formed an independent political force. Criterion 5 does not apply. However, deep ideological tensions have continued to divide the Finns. The civil war left a bitter memory, separating labor from other population segments. There was a strong but ultimately suppressed fascist movement between 1929 and 1933. Clearly Criterion 6 applies. The regime is, and has been since its origin, trichotomized without a right.[34]

Austria first appears as a distinct nation-state at the breakup of the Austro-Hungarian Empire in 1918. This residual German-speaking portion of the former Empire had almost totally different political cultures in its capital city, Vienna, and in the countryside. The Social Democratic party, Marxist and agnostic, was dominant in Vienna. A People's party, based on the Catholic peasantry outside Vienna, had the edge in popular support for the country as a whole. It shortly came to be dominated by extreme conservatives hostile to democracy. The dissension was so extreme that, although the army did not, in fact, play any important political role, Criterion 5 must be considered applicable. Criterion 7 clearly is not applicable. Any generalized liberalism, within which egalitarian socialism might have been subsumed as a mere tendency, was in 1918 long a thing of the past. Moreover, the Populists (whose official position was not undemocratic) and the later fascistic movements were clearly centrist in the terms

[34]Hugh Shearman, *Finland: The Adventures of a Small Power* (London, 1950).

of the criterion. The initial regime in 1918 was thus trichotomized with a right.

Formally, the two parties governed in coalition for the first two years. Thereafter, intransigent hostility was manifest between the Vienna Socialists and the government headed by the People's party. A fascistic movement, the Heimwehr (originally a peasant defense force), was developed in the 1920's under Italian sponsorship. In protesting the acquittal of Heimwehr members who had killed Socialists, a working-class uprising disrupted Vienna for several days in 1927. It was put down by force. Thereafter, a second fascist movement, the Nazis under German sponsorship, complicated the picture. The conflict among Social Democrats, Heimwehr, and Nazis tended to produce chaos. In March of 1933 the Chancellor dispensed with parliament on a technicality, got control of the Heimwehr by a deal with Italy, and set up a disciplined ruling movement called the Fatherland Front. It appears that Criterion 1 then becomes applicable and that the regime was thereafter totalitarian. The Vienna Socialists rebelled against this regime in February 1934, using the working-class public housing in Vienna as a base. They were totally defeated. In 1938 the German Nazi government seized Austria by force and annexed it to Germany.[35]

In 1945 Soviet and Western occupation forces reconstituted Austria as a country. As before 1933, there were only two strong ideological tendencies, now represented by the revived People's and Socialist parties. The Socialists, however, were no longer doctrinaire Marxists and the People's party was no longer under the control of intransigent conservatives. Nevertheless, their followings still probably had little or nothing in common, and the leaders seem to have

[35]Charles A. Gulick, *Austria from Habsburg to Hitler* (2 vols. Berkeley, 1948).

taken for granted that open rivalry would recreate the bitter divisions of the 1920's. Consequently, the leadership groups of the two parties have subsequently settled almost all political questions by private conference and have governed for most of the time in formal coalition. The occupying powers gave the regime its independence in 1955. It is fairly clear that Criterion 5 does not apply. The degree of care taken by the political leadership to prevent the development of divisive issues indicates that Criterion 6 applies. Thus, the regime after 1955 has been trichotomized without a right.

As has earlier been mentioned, Norway was at Level 3 in 1900 and continued at that level until 1935. Thus, while the regime was trichotomized without a right, the country was at Level 3 or in the transitional range to the next higher level. As has been indicated, Belgium was at Level 3 at least as far back as 1880 and has continued at that level well into the present century.[36]

For Japan the time-series in Chapter II indicates that the transitional range from Level 2 to Level 3 occurred in the period 1900 to 1912 and that Level 3 has continued until the present. The transition of regime-classification from dichotomized to trichotomized with a right should thus have occurred before 1912 rather than during World War I, as has been indicated, but neither date has a degree of certainty such as would justify any concern for this discrepancy. The only suitable data for Uruguay indicate for 1963 the transitional range

[36]Although a *da* of 61, normally indicating the transitional range between Level 3 and Level 4 may be computed for 1947 by the preferred method from data in Table 16, 1955 number, *Demographic Yearbook,* estimates for earlier years show such a heavy concentration in the manual portion of the decision-audience that it is possible the transitional range has not yet been reached.

between Level 3 and Level 4.[37] This is compatible with the assumption that the country was at Level 3 throughout most of, or all, the period since 1900. For Costa Rica also suitable data are limited to one year, 1950, when the Level 3 condition is indicated.[38] For Iceland there appear to be no suitable data for determining level. Indications are for Level 3 for Finland in 1950 and 1960 and the transitional range between Level 2 and Level 3 for 1940.[39] For Austria Level 3 is indicated by data for 1951 and the transitional range from Level 3 to Level 4 by data for 1961.[40]

In 1900 four nation-states (outside Latin America) had trichotomized regimes with a right: Denmark (whose history has already been discussed), France, Germany, and Italy. At the end of 1965 there were twelve: France and Italy plus Argentina, Brazil, Chile, Colombia, Ecuador, Greece, Spain, Panama, Portugal, and Venezuela.

Criterion 4 continues to apply in Germany until the clos-

[37]By preferred method, *da* 56 and nonmanual *da* 39 may be computed from Table 13, 1964 number, *ibid.*

[38]By the preferred method, *da* 33 and nonmanual *da* 21 may be computed from Table 15, 1956 number, *ibid.*

[39]By preferred method, *da*'s of 25 for 1940, 46 for 1950, and 56 for 1960 and a manual *da* of 27 for 1950 from Table 12, 1948 number, Table 16, 1956 number, and Table 12, 1964 number, *ibid.*, respectively, and a nonmanual *da* of 29 may be estimated for 1960 by the usual procedures. There are conflicting data for the earlier period. Table 4, *International Statistical Yearbook 1929,* gives *ag* as 78 for 1910 and 74 for 1920, which suggest Level 2; but Shearman, *op. cit.*, gives the percentage of the working force in agriculture in 1910 as 66, indicating a high Level 2 figure for *da* that would be compatible with the assumption that the transitional range between Levels 2 and 3 had been reached by 1917.

[40]By the preferred method, *da*'s of 52 and 63 and nonmanual *da*'s of 27 and 34 for 1951 and 1961 respectively can be computed from Table 15, 1955 number, and Table 13, 1964 number, *Demographic Yearbook.*

ing days of World War I.[41] Since the major claim of the monarchy was its military prowess, the sudden popular realization of defeat caused the collapse of the old institutions in November 1918. An unproclaimed alliance between the moderate leaders of the Social Democratic party and the military command allowed the erection of an effective provisional government and the formal handing over of its authority to a democratically elected constitutional convention early in 1919. Clearly Criterion 5 applies. The regime that followed, generally known as the Weimar Republic, illustrates the fundamental obstacle that main-stem political attitudes place in the way of the successful functioning of democratic institutions. No consensus existed as to social and political values. The industrial working class had its own complex of institutions distinct from those participated in by other social classes. It (and its professionalized leadership cadres) professed an egalitarian value-system, rendered concrete by the symbolism of the Marxian doctrine of ultimate proletarian revolution. While much of the upper leadership of the Social Democratic party was habituated to democratic forms of politics, the blue-collar egalitarian symbolism of their movement isolated them from the upper levels of a population more than usually status-conscious. Seceding from the Social Democrats at the time of the birth of the new regime, a Communist party attracted and held the allegiance of a large fraction of the working class with a message that called for the violent overthrow of the existing order. Under the pressure of the threat of further working-class defections to the Communists, the Social Democratic leaders had no freedom to develop their appeal in ways that might have reached white-collar and other middle-class elements. Much of both

[41]An excellent political history of Germany in the years between wars is S. William Halperin, *Germany Tried Democracy* (New York, 1946).

the elite and the general population remained attached to the aristocratic values of the former regime and treated the Republic with contempt. The large Zentrum, representing the Catholic population, particularly in Southern Germany, had no firm attachment to any special political regime. Pragmatically, they tolerated the democratic Republic without devotion. Except for small liberal and democratic factions, which were crowded out after the first election or two, no elite grouping valued the existing political regime highly except probably the leaders of the Social Democrats. Their avowed egalitarian and socialistic values, however, were little suited to justifying the actual policies the regime pursued and much of the time prevented them from assuming the responsibilities of executive government.

Particularly during the first two years, local movements of working-class character sought to act in social revolutionary fashion. Occasionally they held control of particular localities (especially Munich) for extended periods before being suppressed by regular military forces and the large vigilante bands which then operated with semiofficial sanction. The memory of working-class assertiveness in the period following World War I left a large portion of the population inclined either to support or to tolerate "antiradical" radicalism of a fascistic character. The concomitant growth of the Communists on the one hand and the Nazis on the other eventually produced in 1930 the "negative majority" in the legislature which made democratic government impossible. The regime limped along through the exercise of emergency powers in the name of the senile president, a former general of the Empire. In January 1933 palace intrigue produced a cabinet headed by Adolf Hitler, the Nazi leader. With the police and military thus under restraint, the Nazi armed squads were free to intimidate all other social forces. Within a matter of weeks practically all organizations of significance were either brought under the control of party-designated leaders or suppressed. Criterion 1 thus becomes applicable. The totalitarian regime so created lasted until the extinction of the historic German state in 1945 with the coming together on German soil of invading forces from the East and the West.[42]

The Italian experience up to World War II was similar to that of Germany.[43] The regime before World War I, however, was a constitutional monarchy patterned after that of Great Britain rather than a real monarchy avowedly based on aristocratic values, as in Germany. Deep social unrest and ideological conflict made Criterion 5 applicable even though a series of clever political leaders had left no necessity or opportunity for actual military intervention. Though Italy was technically among the victors, the end of World War I produced endemic local riot and insurrection, as in Germany. The Communist seizure of power had occurred in Russia in 1917 and the same mistake was commonly made in Italy as in Germany of supposing that local social conditions favored the success of an egalitarian social revolutionary movement with blue-collar support. As in Germany, the period from 1918 through 1922 was characterized by local acts by working-class forces of a social revolutionary character, although in Italy no whole cities were occupied by the "reds." A middle-

[42]Although the German Federal Republic, independent since 1955, is not a nation-state in the sense here adopted, we may note that its political leadership has almost totally avoided the revival of the pre-1933 ideological divisions. No criteria apply. The regime is representative-consensual.

[43]Henry Russell Spencer, *Government and Politics of Italy* (Yonkers-on-Hudson, N.Y., 1932), G. Lowell Field, *The Syndical and Corporative Institutions of Italian Fascism* (New York, 1938); Norman Kogan, *Italy and the Allies* (Cambridge, Mass., 1956), and *The Government of Italy* (New York, 1962).

class reaction similar to that in Germany allowed the growth of an anti-egalitarian radical movement. This was eventually brought under the control of Benito Mussolini and styled the Fascist party. In a sort of unofficial civil war (in which the organs of government looked the other way), armed Fascist squads broke up working-class organization more or less completely in the period 1921–1922. Then the Fascists made an open bid for political power. Abandoning the politicians of the old regime, the King, apparently on the urging of the military command, unconstitutionally made Mussolini prime minister in 1922. Full consolidation of Fascist control of society was slower than in Germany. The suppression of all rival organization was only complete in 1926. At that time, Criterion 1 applies and the regime is totalitarian. As in Germany, this regime lasted until the course of World War II eliminated the independence of the country. In 1943, with the Western Allies invading Italy from the south and the Germans effectively in control of the north, the King and the military command sought to repudiate the Fascist regime, but upon their almost immediate flight to the south it was revived by the Germans and survived in the north until Allied forces completed the occupation of the country in 1945.

Italy was released from Allied tutelage in 1947 with a republican regime closely patterned after the pre-War French Third Republic. Although the Fascists no longer had a significant following, deep ideological division continued to deprive the regime of legitimacy. Initially, at least, Criterion 5 must be considered applicable. Thus, the regime was again trichotomized with a right. Successive elections have, however, by now shown rather conclusively that, although social revolutionary forces (the Communists and until recently a major Socialist faction) draw large support, they are obviously and reliably in a minority. Therefore it would appear that a moderate or conservative administration may be maintained indefinitely on the basis of democratic representative procedures. As this becomes more and more assured, Criterion 5 will no longer apply since there will be no possible incentive for military intervention. Perhaps that point has already been reached. If so, there can be no doubt that ideological division remains acute enough so that Criterion 6 applies. Thus if, or when in the immediate future, the Italian regime is no longer trichotomized with a right, it is, or will be, trichotomized without a right.[44]

As has been indicated, France from 1870 until 1940 was under a regime historically identified as the "Third Republic."[45] It was governed by a series of short-lived cabinets reflecting temporary political deals among a variety of political parties and ephemeral factions into which the Chamber of Deputies, elected at four-year intervals, was divided. The nominal head of state, the president of the republic, occupied an institutionally weak office and the head of the active executive, the president of the council of ministers, was more likely to be a skillful broker than a strong political leader because of the coalition nature of all administrations. Radical-egalitarian factions, the Communists and the Socialists, came to

[44]On the extent of strongly felt ideological division still persisting in Italy see, for instance, Joseph LaPalombara, "Italy: Fragmentation, Isolation, Alienation" in Lucian W. Pye and Sidney Verba, eds., *Political Culture and Political Development* (Princeton, 1965), pp. 290–292.

[45]For the political structure, see Walter Rice Sharp, *The Government of the French Republic* (New York, 1938). A variety of works have been written to interpret to persons of other cultures the peculiar ideological tone of French politics arising from the devotion of the fairly conservative petty bourgeoisie to ideas that belong historically to the tradition of the "left." David Schoenbrun, *As France Goes* (New York, 1957), and Andre Siegfried, *France: A Study in Nationality* (New Haven, 1930), may be suggested.

occupy about a third of the representation in the Chamber. Roughly another third belonged to remnants of the historical "left," still vigorously professing the "radicalism" of 1789 but, as has been remarked, while carrying their hearts on the left, they kept their pocketbooks on the right. The rest of the political spectrum was more highly conservative and less devoted to the cult of the "little man," but by the present century mostly committed verbally to some variety of a historically "leftist" rather than "rightist" ideological position. Ideological divisions were acute enough so that there is no doubt that Criterion 5 applies, but given the combination of weak leadership in the democratic phase of government and a comfortable position for the traditional right within the bureaucracy, civil and military, no occasion for actual military intervention seems to have occurred. Criterion 7 clearly had long ceased to apply. Although (mainly because of the historical circumstances which largely excluded professing Catholics from popular politics) there was no obvious "center" in the sense of the criterion, the radical-egalitarian trends, in spite of customary rhetoric, were not confused with the generalized "leftism" of the petty and upper bourgeoisie.

The Third Republic ended in the German conquest of 1940. When France was liberated by the course of World War II in 1944, the more conservative organizations were discredited by charges of collaboration with the Germans and the radical-egalitarian left, particularly the Communists, had a higher than normal acceptance because of their role in the Resistance. Moreover, Resistance activity had finally allowed the emergence of Catholic political leadership other than that associated with the extreme right. The dominant forces immediately after the War thus consisted of an uneasy combination of the Communists, the Socialists, and the Popular Republican Movement. The latter consisted of moderate or leftist Catholics. It had a short-lived prominence due to receiving the support of most of the petty and upper bourgeoisie, whose own organizations were temporarily in disarray. These political forces organized the Fourth Republic.[46] It was essentially like the Third in that governmental responsibility rested on a rapidly changing series of weak cabinets reflecting coalitions of the varied partisan groupings in the legislature. Moreover, once the inclusion of the Communists in the governing coalitions terminated in 1946, the political line-up also was similar to that in the Third Republic.

Pure lack of authority to govern caused the Fourth Republic to collapse in 1958.[47] The occasion was a double rebellion. The Moslem population of Algeria had been in insurrection since 1954. In 1958 the European settlers, backed by the troops stationed in Algeria, also defied the government on the suspicion that it contemplated yielding to the Moslems. Under the circumstances, it was generally expected that the military would also seek to take control in the home area of France. In France such a clear confrontation of democratic and authoritarian, populistic and elitist values would almost certainly have provoked civil war. This eventuation was avoided because of the availability of a political leader of sufficiently ambiguous identification as to be acceptable to the moderates of all factions. General de Gaulle had led the forces of the "external resistance" during World War II and had headed the initial post-War provisional government. As an army officer and practicing Catholic, he fitted the French stereotype of a conservative, a "man of the right." As the restorer of republican government and one who had re-

[46]Philip Williams, *Politics in Post-War France* (London, New York, Toronto, 1955).

[47]Roy C. Macridis and Bernard E. Brown, *The De Gaulle Republic* (Homewood, Ill., 1960).

tired from politics in 1946 rather than forcibly defy the representatives of the Nation, he might pass as something less than a thoroughgoing authoritarian. The Fifth Republic was organized essentially as a vehicle through which General de Gaulle could rule France. Its constitution now provides for a popularly elected president with practically unlimited discretionary power to deal with "emergencies," but ostensibly leaves normal governance to a cabinet responsible to the legislature. So far, it has been de Gaulle's personal government, but there has been no suppression of opposition forces, and elections have been held regularly. Moreover, the major measures by which the Algerian crisis was liquidated were endorsed by successive plebiscites, and the voters on two occasions elected legislatures with majorities willing, for the most part, to tolerate de Gaulle's dominance of policy and decisions. Thus French voters, like those of Italy, seem reliably inclined to support fairly conservative forces in spite of the vigorous appeals made by strong organizations of the left. Sooner or later, if this trend continues, Criterion 5 should cease to apply, but the surviving ideological divisions, if this should happen in the near future, would certainly make Criterion 6 applicable. Since stable majority support for a clearly organized conservative movement has lasted only eight years in France, as against twenty years in Italy, it would seem a bit premature to raise the question for France whether Criterion 5 has already ceased to apply.

It has been indicated that Spain probably still had a dichotomized regime at the beginning of the twentieth century, that is, that Criterion 7 still applied. This would mean that radical-egalitarian trends then showed insufficient organizational strength to be clearly distinguished in political thinking from the generalized socially critical left. The system of arranged elections and successive Conservative and Liberal majorities, however, broke down as new interests forced their way into representation locally. By the time of World War I, Parliament was capable of being a considerable embarrassment to the regime as well as to the landed oligarchy. In 1923 the military, at least nominally with royal approval, seized power to stop a parliamentary investigation of military scandals. A dictatorship was exercised until 1930 by General Primo de Rivera. The egalitarian left was by this time distinct and, in fact, the Socialists were somewhat favored by the regime in its search for some kind of basis for popular support. Criterion 7 evidently does not apply by the time of the 1923 coup. The regime by then was trichotomized with a right.

Primo de Rivera was quite unsuccessful in attempts to institutionalize his regime.[48] Parliament could not be recalled in its old form. No plausible substitute was found. Eventually in 1930 the King was able to dismiss the dictator and appoint a wholly nondescript regime whose aims and intentions remained in doubt. Municipal elections in 1931 showed large republican successes. This event undermined what traditional authority remained. The King fled the country and a provisional government, consisting of various previously somewhat obscure figures committed to democracy, took over. Quite clearly, such a change could hardly have been generally and unambiguously accepted by the country. Thus, as Criterion 4 ceases to apply, Criterion 5 becomes applicable. The regime continued trichotomized with a right. National elections were held and a republican regime using a cabinet system was organized.

Quite aside from the fact that its very form was unacceptable to many traditionalists, the representative institutions

[48]Frank E. Manuel, *The Politics of Modern Spain* (New York, 1938); A. Ramos Oliveira, *op. cit.*

of the Republic disclosed deep divisions of opinion and interest. Cabinets supported by egalitarian factions associated with remnants of the generalized liberal left governed from 1931 to 1933 and again after 1936, while the intervening regime from 1933 to 1936 was highly conservative in social policy. Thus, the Spanish Republic actually displayed the normally imaginary characteristic sometimes attributed by hostile critics to popular government, namely, that successive elections set up administrations that undertake outright to repeal the policies of their predecessors.[49] When the left won again in the 1936 elections, a major mutiny of military forces brought on a large-scale civil war in which the German Nazis and the Italian Fascists openly intervened on the side of the rebels. In 1938 the last territory held by the Republican government was absorbed by the military regime under General Francisco Franco.

While the military mutiny which originated the Franco regime in 1936 promptly absorbed a substantial already existing fascist movement, the Falange, and made it in a sense an official ruling party, there seems never to have been a complete imposition of a single official ideology. Various conservative viewpoints, particularly those associated with the Catholic Church hierarchy, continued to find effective expression at least in elite circles. Thus, Criterion 1 does not apply. Criterion 5 thus continues to apply and the regime is still trichotomized with a right.

In Portugal also attempts to establish democratic government were unsuccessful in the first half of the twentieth century. In 1910 the monarchy was overthrown. A com-

[49]Why this does not occur in reasonably effective representative systems is best explained in Arthur W. Macmahon, "Conflict, Consensus, Confirmed Trends, and Open Choices," *American Political Science Review,* XLII (1948), 1–15.

pletely chaotic republic, reminiscent of that in Spain in the 1860's, lasted from 1910 to 1926. There were six presidents, forty prime ministers, and two hundred cabinet ministers. In all political changes the action of the military was crucial. Factions playing some role in the routine politics of riot and insurrection ranged to the far egalitarian left. By the end, if not at the beginning, of the Republican period, Criterion 7 no longer applies. In 1926 a military revolt suppressed representative institutions. In 1932 a civilian, Dr. Antonio de Oliveira Salazar, was made prime minister and the following year he instituted what was called a "corporative" state. Ostensibly, Salazar has since been the dominant figure in the regime, but a military man has always been president. While traditionalist and authoritarian, the regime, like that of Spain, seems to fall short of fully satisfying Criterion 1. Its origins support the assumption that Criterion 5 still applies. Hence it is trichotomized with a right.

As in the cases of Spain and Portugal, Criterion 7 seems to have ceased to apply to the regime in Greece fairly early in the present century. By the 1930's the Communists had become familiar as a strong, if distinctly minority, political force, capable of electing a number of members of Parliament. Greek politics had been characterized in the 1920's by a series of *coups d'état*. Several kings, military figures, and a civilian leader, Eleutherios Venezelos, pursued each other in and out of power. Clearly Criterion 5 applies. In 1935 the turn of the wheel resulted in a king who allowed his prime minister, Metaxas, to become a dictator. In this posture Greece was eventually overrun by the Germans in World War II. At the liberation in 1944 the monarchy was again restored without the dictatorship, but the Communists, who had become organizationally strong through participation in the Resistance, sought control in a civil war that lasted from

1947 to 1949. Given the dissidence of the civil war period and subsequent disputes in electoral campaigns and over their results, there seems no reason to doubt that Criterion 5 applies. However, government has been carried on by cabinets reflecting parliamentary majorities most of the time, and military intervention has not, in fact, occurred.

Criterion 5 clearly applied in 1900 to the Latin American countries mentioned above as now having trichotomized regimes with a right except Panama, which did not then exist. In Argentina the basic political fact was the conflict between landed conservatives, who had steadily held power since the middle of the nineteenth century through an oligarchical system based on controlled elections, and the precursors of the later "Radicals," who occasionally rebelled unsuccessfully.[50] In Colombia a bitter rivalry between two hereditary upper-class factions, the landed and clerical Conservatives and the more commercial and anticlerical Liberals, was firmly imprinted on the national consciousness by a past history of civil wars.[51] Venezuela had a historical tradition of only the most brutal and personalistic sort of dictatorship, although ruling forces had recently been nominally "Liberal" in the sense of anticlerical. In Brazil the military had clearly been dominant after the overthrow of the monarchy in 1889 (if not before) and continued to be dominant even though the developing custom of alternating the holding of federal power between two regional oligarchies allowed some semblance of constitutional rule. In Ecuador a typical Liberal versus Conservative factionalism was endemic in the nineteenth century. Clerical forces dominated until 1895. Then began the rule of various military-backed "Liberal" factions.

[50]Peter G. Snow, *Argentine Radicalism* (Iowa City, 1965).

[51]John D. Martz, *Colombia: A Contemporary Political Survey* (Chapel Hill, N.C., 1962).

In Chile also a rivalry of traditionalistic and aristocratic Conservatives with more democratic Liberals was well established during the nineteenth century.[52] It had subsided to some extent in the last decade with the development of a plutocratic parliamentary system in which, in contrast with the usual Latin American practice, frequently changing cabinets, rather than strong presidents, conducted the administration.

With the possible exception of Chile, Criterion 5 is still applicable to these countries in 1965. In Argentina open military rule lasted from the *coup d'état* of 1930 through the Perón period until Arturo Frondizi was allowed to take office as elected president in 1958. He was, however, deposed in 1962, and subsequent administrations obviously have existed at the sufferance of the military leaders. After protracted civil war in the first decade of the century, Colombia gave some appearance of constitutional stability while the Conservatives won all elections until that of 1930. When that election showed a Liberal popular majority, Conservatives abstained from voting until a Liberal split offered them the opportunity to return to office in 1946. Extreme civil strife became endemic after the assassination of a Liberal leader in 1948. The Liberals found it impossible because of violence to contest the election of 1949. The Conservative extremist then elected was displaced by a military dictatorship in 1953. The dictator was overthrown in 1957, and serious efforts were made to tone down the violence of the traditional political struggle by a formal undertaking for the two traditional parties to share power for sixteen years. Endemic politically oriented brigandage, however, continues in the countryside, and dissident factions of each party continually challenge the legitimacy of the 1957 agreement. Ven-

[52] Federico G. Gil, *The Political System of Chile* (Boston, 1966).

ezuela had a short period of more or less popular representative politics from 1935 to 1948, followed by a highly repressive dictatorship lasting until 1958. Subsequently, representative government has been maintained, but it is clearly unrealistic to suppose that Criterion 5 is no longer applicable. In Brazil the polite alternation of power between regional oligarchies was upset by the Vargas dictatorship from 1930 to 1945. Subsequently, fairly representative politics prevailed with one short period of relatively limited military intervention (ostensibly and apparently actually to ensure a fair election) until 1964. Then the overthrow of President Goulart was followed by overt military government. Ecuador had a brief period of plausible constitutional government from 1948 to 1961 preceded and followed by continuous more or less open dominance of government by the military. Panama, formed by secession from Colombia in 1903, was under at least a formal United States protectorate until 1936. Thereafter, political events have been almost entirely determined by the National Police, there being no army so called.

Of the seven Latin American countries now under discussion, it is only in respect to Chile that one may seriously raise the question of the nonapplicability of Criterion 5. There has been regular constitutional government in the present century except for the rule of Carlos Ibañez del Campo from 1924 to 1932, first as minister of war and then as president, and for events of the latter year. There were three irregular seizures of power in 1932, but a constitutional succession of elected presidents extends from 1933 to the present.

While Criterion 7 probably applies in all these cases in 1900, the clear differentiation of a radical-egalitarian left or the formation of "centrist" forces, having partly traditional and partly reformist appeals, or both have subsequently occurred in all cases. In Argentina socialists have been present in the Buenos Aires region since the late nineteenth century. They received 8 per cent of the popular vote for president in 1916 and 9 per cent in 1922. A center, moreover, is visible with the joining of the Conservatives and the Anti-Personalist Radicals in the 1928 election. Criterion 7 probably ceases to apply in Argentina as early as the 1916 elections, the first that involved the secret ballot and other protections for the nonconservative voter. In Colombia, in spite of the continued prominence of the two traditional parties, Criterion 7 probably ceases to apply about 1940. At that time the Communists got control of a fairly substantial labor organization. Shortly thereafter, a Church-affiliated labor organization became prominent, manifesting a centrist trend. Moreover, the Rojas Pinilla dictatorship from 1953 to 1957 also had a centrist character. The criterion becomes inapplicable about 1940 in Venezuela also. Since 1940 there has been a clearly differentiated proletarian left as well as organized parties of centrist type, particularly the Christian Democratic COPEI and the Accion Democrática. In Brazil the populistic appeal of the Vargas dictatorship on social questions combined with the conservative association provided by its military character marks it as clearly centrist in the sense of the criterion. Probably the criterion ceases to apply with Vargas' seizure of power in 1930. The radical-egalitarian left seems to have been clearly recognized in Ecuadorean politics since the early 1940's, even though the still limited suffrage reduces its effectiveness. As from 1944 at least, the extreme left is as likely to support nominal Conservatives as Liberals, an indication of centrism. The center is obvious in Chile with the overthrow of President Alessandri by his war minister, Carlos Ibañez del Campo, who offered the same combination of conservative military associations with populistic appeals as Perón, Vargas, Rojas Pinilla, and Primo de Rivera. Moreover, shortly thereafter the proletarian left appears among the factions regularly represented in the legislature. In Panama the original Liberal-Conservative line-up inherited from Colombia disintegrated in the first decade of national existence. Centrist and radical-egalitarian tendencies have since been clearly present.

Of the fourteen nation-states mentioned as having had trichotomized regimes with a right during the period from 1900 to 1965, the levels for two have been fully set forth in Chapter II. Germany was at Level 3 from some time before 1882 until 1933, when it seems to have entered the transitional range between Levels 3 and 4. Italy has been continuously at Level 3 from before 1871 until the present time. It has already been noted that France was at Level 3 before 1900. It probably remained at this level until the 1950's, when it entered the transitional range between Level 3 and Level 4.[53] Isolated data for 1947 only indicate that Argentina probably had reached the transitional range above Level 3 by that date.[54] Similarly isolated data for Brazil for 1950 indicate the transitional range below Level 3.[55] Chile appears to have been at Level 3 in 1952 and to have reached the transitional range between Level 3 and Level 4 about 1960.[56] For Colombia

[53]For 1962 a *da* of 61 and a nonmanual *da* of 32 can be computed from data in Table 13, 1964 number, *Demographic Yearbook*. This is clearly in the transitional range from Level 3 to Level 4. If *ac* was already reduced to the 1962 level of approximately 20 in 1954, one may estimate a *da* of 53, also in the transitional range, for 1954 from data in Table 12, 1954 number, *ibid*. If *ac* was then much higher, Level 3 may still have prevailed at that date.

[54]A *da* of 52 can be computed by the preferred method from data in Table 16, 1955 number, *ibid*.

[55]A *da* of 25 may be computed by the preferred method from data in Table 16, 1956 number, *ibid*.

[56]A *da* of 45 may be computed by the preferred method for 1952 from data in Table 15, 1956 number, *ibid*. A *da* of 50 and a nonmanual *da*

evidence as to level is somewhat conflicting, but it seems probable that the transitional range between Level 2 and Level 3 was attained in the 1930's and that Level 3 was attained in the 1950's.[57] This would be compatible with the earlier reported shift from a dichotomized regime to a trichotomized regime with a right about 1940. Data for Ecuador indicate a probable regression from a clear Level 3 condition around 1950 to the range transitional between Level 2 and Level 3, perhaps about 1958.[58] For Greece also data indicate a probable regression about 1956 from Level 3 to the transitional range between Level 2 and Level 3.[59] Isolated data for 1920 indicate that Spain was probably in the transitional range between Level 2 and Level 3 at that time.[60] Panama appears to have been in the transitional range between Level 2 and Level 3 in recent years.[61] Portugal has been clearly at

---

of 31 may be similarly computed for 1960 from data in Table 13, 1964 number, *ibid.*

[57]Table 13, 1949–50 number, *ibid.* gives *ag* as 74 for 1938. Computation by the preferred method on these data yields a low Level 2, i.e., *da* 10. However, John M. Hunter, *Emerging Colombia* (Washington, 1962) includes data showing *ag* as 66 for 1925, 60 for 1945, and 52 for 1958. Estimating *da*'s from these data by the usual procedures indicates the levels given in the text.

[58]The *da* computed by the preferred method drops from 32 in 1950 to 18 in 1962 on the basis of data from Table 15, 1956 number, and Table 12, 1964 number, *Demographic Yearbook* respectively, because of a sharp increase in both given *ag* and computed *ac*. In the first case a nonmanual *da* of 15 can be computed by the preferred method. This drops to 10 in 1962 when estimated by the usual procedures (data in this case being industrial).

[59]Computation by the preferred method gives *da* 25 and nonmanual *da* 15 for 1961 on the basis of data in Table 13, 1964 number, *ibid.* Table 12, 1956 number, gives *ag* 48 for 1951. Estimated *da,* assuming *ac* at 16, is 36. If *ac* is taken as 20 (it was 21 in 1961), *da* was 32.

[60]A *da* of 25 may be estimated for 1920 by the usual procedure from data in Table 4, *International Statistical Yearbook 1929.*

[61]Computed by the preferred method, *da* is 32 for 1950 and 35 for

Level 3 in recent decades.[62] Venezuela was at Level 3 about 1950 and reached the transitional range between Level 3 and Level 4 about 1958.[63]

In 1900 seven nation-states (aside from those in Latin America) had dichotomized regimes. These were Greece, Japan, Portugal, Serbia, Spain, Romania, and Russia. None of these had regimes of this kind in 1965. However, there were still eight Western nation-states with dichotomized regimes in 1965, all Latin American. These were Bolivia, the Dominican Republic, Guatemala, Honduras, Nicaragua, Paraguay, Peru, and El Salvador. The recent political histories of Greece, Japan, Portugal, and Spain have already been sketched. As has been indicated, Japan was, and the other three could have been, below Level 3 when they had dichotomized regimes.

Serbia was expanded after World War I and in 1929 assumed the name Yugoslavia. It was a real monarchy with chaotic (nominally parliamentary) politics until 1929, after which the monarch exercized dictatorial powers. Although briefly securing some representation in Parliament in 1920, the extreme left seems to have had little secure organization-

1960 (values normally in Level 3), but manual *da* is only 9 for 1950 and 8 for 1960. Data are from Table 15, 1956 number, and Table 13, 1964 number, *Demographic Yearbook,* respectively. Here is a case of abnormally high nonmanual *da* in a commercial entrepot, making our conventional *da* cutting points unreliable, as abnormally high manual *da*'s tend to do in several countries with much manufacture.

[62]Computed by the preferred method, *da* is 40 in 1940, 40 in 1950, and 44 in 1960 and nonmanual *da* is 23 in the latter year. Data are from Table 12, 1948 number, Table 16, 1955 number, Table 13, 1964 number, *ibid.,* respectively.

[63]Computed by the preferred method, *da* was 37 in 1950 and 43 in 1961 while nonmanual *da* was 24 in 1950 and 33 in 1961. Data are from Table 15, 1956 number, and Table 13, 1964 number, *ibid.,* respectively. This is another case of abnormally high nonmanual *da* making the estimate of level by *da* misleading.

al strength until World War II. The Germans overran the country and drove out the royal government in 1941. Two resistance forces operated against the Germans and against each other. One of these, led by Communists, came into control of the country when the German power collapsed. Because of the official Communist doctrine, Criterion 1 clearly applied to this regime as soon as it controlled territory. Initially, Criterion 3 (the revolutionary case) may also have applied and the regime may have been temporarily radical-egalitarian. Shortly, however, normal bureaucratic organization is clear, so that Criterion 3 could only have applied briefly after the war. Thus, the regime in Yugoslavia has been totalitarian since at least as early as 1949. Data for 1931 indicate Level 2, while those for 1953 indicate the transitional range between Level 2 and Level 3.[64]

Criteria 4 and 7 first applied in the case of Romania. Political power rested with the throne and the military, but some representative politics, reflected in a cabinet system, took place.[65] Until World War II, political forces did not include either a strongly organized egalitarian left or clear centrist forces. After the death of King Ferdinand in 1927, the incumbency of the throne alternated twice between King Michael and his father, King Carol. Probably Criterion 5 rather than Criterion 4 is applicable after 1927. Having allied with the Germans in World War II, Romania was overrun by Russian troops in 1944. A "people's republic" was organized in 1947. Like the other puppet states in Eastern Europe after World War II, Romania remained for a time a *de facto*

[64]Computed by the preferred method, *da* was 12 in 1931 and 28 in 1953 on the basis of data from Table 12, 1948 number, and Table 16, 1955 number, *ibid.*, respectively.

[65]See Joseph S. Roucek, *The Politics of the Balkans* (New York and London, 1939).

dependency of the Soviet Union. Just when this status terminated is difficult to determine. However, by 1963 it is clear that Criterion 2 no longer applies to Romania in view of a rather sharp and open diplomatic disagreement with the Soviet Union. With most of the Russian troops withdrawn from the area and with the Russians in a situation (particularly because of Chinese propaganda attacks) where forcible intervention would be very inexpedient, the same year may also be taken as marking *de facto* independence for the Russian satellites in Eastern Europe other than East Germany. Clearly in the case of Romania, by 1963 only Criterion 1 applies and the regime is totalitarian. Romania in the period just before World War II was at Level 2. At present it seems to have reached Level 3.[66]

Russia was an absolute monarchy in 1900 and, although a weak representative body, the Duma, existed after the 1905 upheavals, there was no essential shift of power from the royal court until the Revolution in 1917.[67] Thus Criterion 4 applies. Criterion 7 also applies. The attitude of the dominant bureaucracy made practically no distinction between egalitarian radicals and the most moderate liberals and, in the very weak state of organization of subversive forces before 1917, it would have been difficult for any one else to draw the distinction sharply.

Russia in the 1917–1921 period went through essentially the same kind of collapse of the previous social order as had England in the winter of 1648–1649 and France in 1792–1794

[66]Computed by the preferred method, *da* is 14 in 1930 and 26 in 1960. However, estimated by the usual procedure, manual *da* is 14 in the latter year. Data are from Table 13, 1949–50 number, and Table 12, 1964 number, *Demographic Yearbook,* respectively.

[67]George A. Vernadsky, *op. cit.*

but with a different outcome.[68] Participation in World War I demanded economic and social mobilization on a scale that the old Russian state was unable to accomplish. Supply difficulties, food shortages, military defeats, and mass desertions of troops brought the authority of the monarchy to an end in March 1917. Some riots in the capital, in which troops joined, signalled the change. Since the Duma had been so elected as to overrepresent the upper classes heavily, it lacked authority to take over power from the monarchy. Improvisation of institutions was necessary. The bureaucratic services and the foreign diplomatic representation were taken over by a provisional government representing a wide range of liberal, democratic, and mildly radical tendencies. Working-class strata in the cities were promptly organized by more radical political cadres into a *de facto* representative system heading up in councils or "soviets," which found themselves taking over the essential administration of local matters because of the vacuum of authority. The troops at the front remained under the control of officers for the most part so

[68]A book of very high quality which compares in detail the major revolutions (English, French, and Russian, incongruously along with the very different American Revolution) is Crane Brinton's *The Anatomy of Revolution* (New York, 1952). The studies leading to the present work were originally undertaken to a large extent with a view to "generalizing" Brinton's theory of revolution. We eventually reached the conclusion that it is one of the great illusions of the present age (a delusion that has mislead many scholars) that there is anything in the theory of "revolutions" to generalize. These three great national events are practically unique. They occur in classic form only because of the almost incredible stupidity of previous rulers. The West has seen no other cases and it is doubtful that the East will see any. Equivalent transformations, of course, occur as a result of invasion and conquest by foreign forces, as happened at the end of World War II in Eastern Europe. It is, however, practically impossible for domestic forces (as in the three classic cases) fully to undermine the authority of existing elites as a whole.

reactionary as to be unable to accept the democratic aspirations of the provisional government although for the moment they submitted nominally to its authority. Garrison troops at home threw out their officers, elected committees to replace them, and joined in the working-class soviet movement. The countryside fell to strictly local peasant movements, which seized all land and destroyed land records.

It is difficult to decide the exact extent of the polity to be described in the period following the March 1917 Revolution, but it consisted essentially of the cities of Russia as a collective entity. In most cities the formal authority of the provisional government was accepted, but actual administration by workers' and soldiers' councils was set up almost immediately after the March upheaval in the capital. Since there was widespread and almost chaotic expression of a variety of political views, Criterion 1 does not apply to this regime. Criterion 3 seems not to apply until the second upheaval in November since, for the most part, the various bureaucratic services continued in operation. In the almost total lack of established authority, Criterion 5 obviously applies, although there were rather few bodies of troops in the interior under any serious control by officers. Criterion 7 still applies. The contrast between the stark traditionalism of the old regime, still largely represented by the officer corps, and an undifferentiated range of socially critical opinions was probably reinforced rather than undermined by the initial experience of freedom to propose and to discuss political measures. Moreover, political movements seeking mass followings were only for the first time actively engaged in propagating their views. For the most part, the population had not yet been reached. The accident that no channels for representative politics existed except the working-class soviets (originally conceived of as organs of class representation in lieu of nonexistent trade unions) gave great advantage to the propagandists of various forms of working-class radicalism.

The provisional government sought to hold out until elections, scheduled for November, could produce a constitutional convention having authority on the basis of popular choice. It was unable to do so, particularly because it sought to continue effective Russian participation in the war. This was highly unpopular and practically impossible. A small band of disciplined Marxian revolutionaries, called the Bolshevik wing of the Social Democratic party (the later "Communists"), saw the opportunity the organization of the politically ignorant working class in the soviets afforded them at a time when no other channels of representative politics existed. Between March and November, by a gradual process of infiltration and propaganda, they secured leadership of the soviets for themselves in most cities and secured what the early soviet leaders had formally repudiated, a commitment of the soviets to claim legitimate political power. With control of the soviets went leadership of the officerless military forces which had attached themselves to these organs of representation. In November the troops associated with the soviet of the capital seized the ministries and turned over formal control of government to the Bolshevik leaders, who acted nominally as the designees of a convention of delegates from the soviets of various cities. Other cities immediately followed suit. With this action, extreme egalitarian forces were free to demand conformance from the general population. At the same time the old bureaucracy, which the provisional government had taken over essentially intact from the Tsarist government, disintegrated. Criteria 1 and 3 (the revolutionary case) thus apply to the polity comprising the cities of Russia after the November Revolution and the regime is radical-egalitarian.

The regime survived over the next few years primarily because of the political polarization that occurred. Moderate liberals or democrats had no place to go except to politically ineffective exile. They were persecuted as reactionaries by the egalitarian enthusiasts who dominated the streets in the Soviet area. If they reached the peripheries of Russia, where armies, now consisting mostly of former officers, controlled territory, they found themselves regarded by these forces as indistinguishable from their former persecutors. This is essentially what had happened in France in 1792 but had failed to occur to the same degree in England in 1648–1649 because the officers of the existing army were themselves for the most part moderates. In Russia the White Armies, the former imperial forces now reduced mostly to former officers, remained in the field with the support of foreign intervening armies for about four years. They were eventually defeated. Meanwhile, the Communists had rebuilt a centralized administrative structure and a new disciplined army. In 1921 the radical-egalitarian regime ended, as it had in France in 1794 and in England in 1649, with the reassertion of centralized bureaucratic control of coercive power. The sailors at the base at Kronstadt, realizing that they had been taken in by the concept of "working-class democracy," rebelled with the slogan "The soviets without the Communist Party." The regime had troops available to suppress the mutiny. While in the English and French cases the similar event ended the applicability of both Criterion 1 and Criterion 3 and restored the applicability of Criteria 5 and 7, in Russia the only effect was that Criterion 3 ceased to apply. The disciplined Communist party continued to follow a political line from which deviation was not permissible. Therefore, in 1921 the regime in Russia became totalitarian. It has remained such to the present day.

It has already been indicated that Russia was at Level 2

at the turn of the century. Probably this condition persisted until 1917, perhaps prevailed technically after 1921 (inasmuch as the real polity then continuously administered by the Soviet government was confined to the remnant military and bureaucratic populations of the dwindled cities), and was fully restored by about 1928. The widespread devastation of the Civil War from 1918 to 1920 drastically reduced productivity and rendered city life temporarily impossible except for cadres deemed essential by the government. In the 1930's, industrialization and the elimination of the remnants of private enterprise probably raised the Level to 3.[69]

For the eight Latin American countries still with dichotomized regimes in 1965, Criterion 5 applies in all cases.[70] In between military regimes, Honduras had one elected civilian president, serving from 1958 to 1963. However, the military stopped the next election when one of the candidates proposed that they should thereafter be subject to the control of the civil government. Although somewhat more popular politics have been practiced in El Salvador since the 1940's, there is no reason to doubt that the military still determine who is to hold office. Administrations normally change by

[69]There are few data suitable for any exact computation of level. S. N. Harper and R. Thompson, *The Government of the Soviet Union* (New York, 1952), p. 178, reproduce figures given in a report to the Eighteenth Party Congress as to the social composition of the population in 1913, 1928, and 1937. If peasants (individual and collective) are taken as *ag*, "exploiting classes" as *ac*, and "workers and employees" as *da* we get:

		ag	*ac*	*da*
1913	–	65	16	19
1928	–	76	5	19
1937	–	61	0	39

[70]A convenient summary treatment of recent Latin American regimes will be found in Lewis Hanke, *Mexico and the Caribbean* (Princeton, 1959), and *South America* (Princeton, 1959).

coups d'état in Peru. There have been two elections, perhaps, in which the military stood aside and allowed a choice by the voters. In each case the term of the elected president was ended by a *coup d'état*. There has been a family dictatorship in Nicaragua since the end of the last United States occupation in 1933. With a slight delay following the United States withdrawal in 1926, the same thing happened in the Dominican Republic. Instability has followed the overthrow of the Trujillo family in 1963. In 1965–1966, pending the outcome of elections, the country was in effect occupied by forces sponsored by the Organization of American States. Bolivia has had a chaotic political history in which no elected president served out his term until 1952. A reformist party managed to hold power from 1952 until 1964, when open military control was resumed. A similar experience in Guatemala led to a regime committed to social reform in 1944. This became more radical, with open participation by Communists, and was overthrown by military intervention in 1954. After nine years of conservative rule, the military again resumed open control in 1963. Except for a few months of what was possibly a radical-egalitarian regime in 1936, Paraguay has been governed by military dictatorships of conservative social policy throughout its history.

The continued application of Criterion 7 until the present time in all these cases is clear. Starkly traditionalist forces are obvious enough so that it is very difficult for moderate liberals and democrats to differentiate themselves clearly, either in their own thinking or in the eyes of others, from radical-egalitarian forces which appear to be "on the same side." Thus, Communist infiltration of the more or less open kind that occurred in the Abenz regime in Guatemala is always a possibility when the conservatives are not in power. Reformist groupings in Bolivia, the Dominican Republic, and Guatemala and probably in the other countries of this group are under a deep temptation to ally closely with radical-egalitarians in the attempt to build up forces sufficient to keep the traditionalists out of power. This is a basic characteristic of dichotomized as contrasted with trichotomized regimes.

In all these eight cases there are data for at least one fairly recent year indicative of attained level and all such data are compatible with the assumption that dichotomized regimes occur at Level 2 or at one of the two adjacent transitional ranges. Bolivia, the Dominican Republic, Guatemala, Nicaragua, and Paraguay were all at Level 2 in 1950.[71] Two dates suggest trends for the other three countries. Honduras shows an advance from the transitional range between Level 1 and Level 2 in 1950 to full Level 2 in 1961.[72] El Salvador holds steady in 1950 and 1961 in the transitional range between Level 2 and Level 3.[73] Peru seems to have risen from Level 2 in 1940 to the transitional range from Level 2 to Level 3 in 1961.[74]

Given the limitation of "Western nation-states" that was set on the historical examples to be discussed, there has turned up only one example of a regime to which both Cri-

[71]Full computation by preferred method is from Table 15, 1956 number, *Demographic Yearbook,* for Guatemala and Paraguay. Computation of *da* only by preferred method is from Table 16, 1955 number, for Bolivia and Nicaragua. Estimate of *da* by usual procedure is from Table 13, 1956 number, for the Dominican Republic.

[72]Full computation for both years is by preferred method, Table 15, 1956 number, and Table 13, 1964 number, *ibid.,* respectively.

[73]Full computation for 1950 by preferred method is from Table 15, 1956 number, *ibid.* Computation of *da* for 1961 by preferred method and estimation of nonmanual *da* by usual procedure are from Table 12, 1964 number.

[74]Computation of *da* only by preferred method for 1940 is from Table 12, 1948 number, *ibid.* Full computation for 1961 by preferred method is from Table 13, 1964 number.

terion 5 and Criterion 3 apply and which therefore can be classified as a traditional regime. This is Haiti. Its classification seems to have remained unchanged (except for a period of United States occupation) since the beginning of the century. After some grandiose and perhaps partly mythological rulers in the early nineteenth century and except for a United States occupation from 1915 to 1934, Haiti seems to have been continuously governed by a series of rather weak military dictatorships. Holding of power is determined by what military forces happen to exist. Hence Criterion 5 clearly applies. Although the city population tends to monopolize preferred occupations, they are not landed and do not dominate the back country. It seems doubtful that the rural areas are very systematically or continuously administered, although there would normally be no question of the power of the central authorities to dominate any particular area by force if necessary. Hence Criterion 3 appears to apply. No data suitable for the indication of level for Haiti have been found by the present writer.

While there were no totalitarian regimes at the beginning of the century, in 1965 there were nine such among Western nation-states. The Soviet Union, Romania, and Yugoslavia have already been discussed. The others are Albania, Bulgaria, Cuba, Czechoslovakia, Hungary, and Poland. Like Romania, four of these—Bulgaria, Czechoslovakia, Hungary, and Poland—became totalitarian regimes while Russian troops dominated their territory at the end of World War II.

Bulgaria secured full independence from Turkey in 1908. It was ruled by a monarch with some degree of popular representation. Criteria 4 and 7 applied and the regime was dichotomized. A social-reformist peasant faction was dominant from 1919 to 1926. Although Communists and Socialists appear among factions represented in the 1920's, there is nothing to indicate that the general right-left stereotype of dichotomized regimes was modified. There was a royal dictatorship in the late 1930's, followed by involvement in World War II and Russian occupation after 1944. A "people's democracy" was then set up. As in other cases of Russian satellites, substantial independence of Russia may be presumed from about 1963. Clearly, only one of the criteria, Criterion 1, applies. In the 1930's Bulgaria was only in the transitional range between Level 1 and Level 2. In 1956 it seems to have attained Level 3.[75]

Czechoslovakia came into existence in 1918 with the disintegration of the Austro-Hungarian Empire. Criteria 1 through 4 were not applicable. Although there was very serious ideological division, the institutional pattern seems to have been respected, and there is no indication of a military role in politics. Hence, although Criterion 5 was not applicable, Criterion 6 evidently was and the regime was trichotomized without a right. This polity was brought under German control by force in 1938 and was ruled as a dependency until 1945. With liberation came substantial Russian control. It seems to have been generally understood by the liberal democratic leaders of the revived polity that Russia would not allow more than a limited degree of independence to them. They could only hope that this limited degree extended to a non-Communist regime. Although Communists initially made no attempt at a take-over, it was necessary to allow them to participate in the governing coalition, and it was not possible to take serious steps to block their infiltra-

[75]Computed by the preferred method, *da* was 9 in 1934 and 33 in 1956. Estimated by the usual procedures, nonmanual *da* was 16 in the latter year. See Table 12, 1948 number, and Table 12, 1964 number, *ibid.*, respectively.

tion of strategic positions. From 1945 to 1948 only Criterion 2 applies and the regime was dependent trichotomized. In 1948 the Communists took full control of the government by semirevolutionary procedures. It appears that the leaders of the regime felt that only token opposition could be offered. Criterion 1 applies from 1948. As with other ex-satellites, 1963 may be taken as the date when Criterion 2 ceased to apply and the regime changed from dependent totalitarian to totalitarian. Czechoslovakia was at Level 3 in the 1920's. It seems to have risen to the transitional range between Level 3 and Level 4 after World War II.[76]

Poland was also re-created in the aftermath of World War I. It had a developed radical-egalitarian left, some centrist forces, and a relatively political military establishment. Hence Criterion 5 applied but Criterion 7 did not and the regime was trichotomized with a right. Degenerating ultimately into a tight dictatorship, this regime was destroyed by German invasion in 1938. The country was ruled harshly as a dependency until 1944, when Russian occupying forces replaced German. The regime until 1947, like that in Czechoslovakia, was dependent trichotomized (Criterion 2 only applicable). In that year all opposition to Communism wa suppressed and a "people's democracy" established. As in Hungary, serious popular unrest eventuated in demonstrations and riots in 1956. The Polish Communists, with a change in leadership, managed to keep control, making limited concessions to liberal sentiment in certain sections of the population. These changes did not open the way to any real multifactionalism. They did, however, place the

[76]Estimated by the usual procedure, *da* was around 43 in 1920. Computed by the preferred method, *da* was 51 in 1947. For 1920, see Table 4, *International Statistical Yearbook 1929;* for 1947, Table 16, 195[illegible] number, *Demographic Yearbook.*

regime in a stance of rather sharp opposition to Russian wishes. Criterion 1 continues applicable through 1956, but Criterion 2 ceases to apply and the regime changed from dependent totalitarian to totalitarian. Poland seems still to have been in the transitional range between Level 2 and Level 3 in the early 1930's. In 1960 it had attained Level 3.[77]

Hungary, like Austria and Czechoslovakia, came into existence following the disintegration of Austria-Hungary in 1918. It experienced a brief radical-egalitarian regime (Criteria 1 and 3—revolutionary case—being applicable), which was suppressed by Romanian troops, and then passed into the hands of remnants of its own military forces under Admiral Horthy, who ruled as "regent" until World War II. There was a degree of parliamentary politics most of the time and socialists were a clearly differentiated faction. Hence Criterion 5 applies but Criterion 7 does not; the regime in the interwar years was trichotomized with a right. First the Germans and then the Russians took control during World War II. As in Poland and Czechoslovakia, the initial satellite regime was dependent trichotomized (Criterion 2 only applicable), followed after 1949, when all opposition to Communism was suppressed, by a dependent totalitarian regime (Criteria 1 and 2 applicable). Popular outbreaks, similar to those in Poland, occurred in 1956; they swept over the country. Before the Russians decided openly to intervene by force, the insurrection had completely paralyzed and disrupted the Communist administration. Only one Criterion, number 3, appears to apply to the brief popular regime. It would, therefore, have to be described as a citizen-community although,

[77]Computed by the preferred method, *da* was 21 in 1931 and 50 in 1960. Estimated by the usual procedure, nonmanual *da* was 22 in the latter year. For 1931, see Table 12, 1948 number, *Demographic Yearbook;* for 1960, Table 12, 1964 number.

except for its being a reaction against a Communist regime of egalitarian pretensions, it very closely resembled a radical-egalitarian regime. Russian troops shortly re-established a dependent totalitarian regime. As with Romania, Czechoslovakia, and Bulgaria it presumably became substantially independent by 1963. Hungary was at Level 3 in 1941 and seems to have just attained the transitional range between Level 3 and Level 4 in 1960.[78]

Albania secured independence from the Turks in 1913. With the evidence available to the present writer, it is difficult to characterize the initial regime. It may have been traditional (Criteria 3 and 5) or dichotomized (Criteria 5 and 7). The country passed under Italian control in the late 1930's. As in Yugoslavia, a native resistance movement under Communist control was allowed to take over at the end of World War II. Thus, like Yugoslavia, Albania was never a *de facto* dependency of the Soviet Union, as were other Communist regimes of Eastern Europe. Whether or not there was originally a radical-egalitarian regime (Criteria 1 and 3), the regime has clearly been for some time totalitarian (Criterion 1 only). No data suitable for the determination of level seem to be available.

The United States protectorate over Cuba was formally terminated in 1934. Criterion 5 applies to the subsequent regime, but Criterion 7 does not. It was thus trichotomized with a right. Ideological difference and the lack of any strong tradition of institutional legitimacy invited military intervention. There was a strong and distinct socialist faction. Colonel Batista, formerly a sergeant, who had led a noncommissioned officers' revolt in 1933, was the dominant fig-

[78]Computed by the preferred method, *da* was 38 in 1941 and 62 in 1960, and nonmanual *da* was 30 in the latter year. Data are found in Table 12, 1948 number, and Table 13, 1964 number, *ibid.*, respectively.

ure in politics from 1934 until 1958, except for the interval of two presidential terms, 1944–1952, which he did not control. This eight-year interval, the best specimen of democratic government in the Cuban experience, was not such as to arouse wide enthusiasm. Initially, Batista had been a sort of Robin Hood. In his second period of power, after 1952, he lost this character rapidly. This regime degenerated into brutal terrorism as the operations of guerillas, centered in the southeastern mountains and led by Fidel Castro, goaded the administration into retaliation. Castro's forces became the idealists' symbol of resistance to an immoral tyranny. Eventually, these forces would go on the offensive in a brief campaign in December 1958. By January 1, 1959, resistance had crumbled, and Castro's appointees were shortly in nominal power in Havana.

Classifying the Castro regime in Cuba at its inception is obviously difficult. The hero did not wish to take a top post immediately. There was no admission of Communistic leanings, and it may even be doubted that Castro was a Communist party member in good standing at the time. If the regime was a Communistic totalitarian dictatorship, it must be admitted that the President, the Prime Minister, and numerous other front-men were unaware of its true character. An alternative is to suppose that the regime was radical-egalitarian. This seems unlikely. The Castro forces were well organized and held full centralized control of the areas they occupied. Perhaps deliberately, the capital city was left out. It seems most plausible that the Castro regime as soon as it controlled any territory to speak of came under Criterion 1 and no other criterion, that Castro stayed away from the government center in Havana at first because it was not yet the real center of his power, and that the government he invited into office was allowed a bit of liberalism merely for show.

At any rate, the phenomenon was brief. By the summer of 1959 one could not quibble; the regime was totalitarian. Data, available for 1953 only, indicate that Cuba was at Level 3 at that time. Presumably, it had been at this level since its release from United States control in 1934.[79]

All types of regimes distinguishable by the criteria introduced in Chapter I except the two Level 1 types, the traditional regime and the citizen-community, appear repeatedly in the foregoing narrative at least in the period after 1900. In a large number of cases, data as to working-force composition independently support the levels with which the different types of regimes are believed to be associated. The limitation to modern Western polities practically eliminated traditional regimes. The limitation to nation-states probably eliminates by definition any really viable cases of citizen-communities. Without this limitation, Andorra might have been cited as an example.

STABILITY OF THE REGIME-TYPES

Previous discussion has shown fairly clearly the high continuity of all three basic regime-types. Except for the massive intrusion of forces based outside the polity in question, as in international war and in highly organized and protracted civil warfare, changes among the three main types of regimes have been exceedingly rare. In the preceding discussion, changes among the three types not coinciding with liberation, conquest, or substantially similar circumstances, what may be called "changes of regime-type in a continuing polity," are limited to the following:

[79]Computed by the preferred method, *da* was 40 and nonmanual *da* 26 on the basis of data in Table 15, 1956 number, *ibid.*

1. Main-stem (dichotomized) to utopian (radical-egalitarian)
   - Scotland, 1639
   - England, 1648
   - France, 1792
   - Russia, 1917
2. Utopian (radical-egalitarian) to main-stem (dichotomized)
   - England, 1649
   - France, 1794
3. Main-stem (trichotomized with right) to utopian (totalitarian)
   - Italy, 1926
   - Germany, 1933
4. Main-stem (dichotomized) to consensual (representative-consensual)
   - England, 1689
   - Sweden, 1809
   - Mexico, 1933
5. *Possibly* in a continuing polity (with close approach of Level 4)—main-stem (trichotomized without right) to consensual (representative-consensual)
   - Denmark, 1933 (?)
   - Norway, about 1935 (?)

Thus, the historical record shows that (at least in modern Western nation-states) the three main regime-types are exceedingly stable. There is, however, a marked difference among the three types in the stability of *individual* regimes, as distinguished from the categories into which such regimes are classified. The stability of representative-consensual regimes and of totalitarian regimes is the stability of the actual regimes. There is no similar stability of actual regimes in the main-stem category except for trichotomized regimes without a right. This distinction may be demonstrated if regimes in the nation-states covered in the previous discussion are classified according to the applicability of Criterion 20 as well as that of Criterion 1 through 7, and if any regime established by an obviously irregular seizure of power (a *coup d'état*) is treated as distinct from its predecessor. Thus, a regime change would be recognized if any change in the applicability of Criteria 1 to 7 occurred, if a *coup d'état* substituted new top governing personnel, if Criterion 20 became applicable (an event fairly likely to coincide with the foregoing), or if Criterion 20 ceased to be applicable (as might occur with a change of administration as the result of an election). All "regimes," counted in this way, existing from the beginning of 1950 through the end of 1965 in the countries dealt with in the preceding narrative have been enumerated. In discussing this enumeration, the term "autocratic" will be added to the usual regime description in cases where Criterion 20 is applicable and "nonautocratic" in cases where it is not. Note that Criterion 20 by its own terms cannot be applied along with either Criterion 1 or Criterion 3. Hence, the distinction will not be made for regimes to which the latter criteria are applicable.

The number of regimes to which Criterion 3 applied is negligible. Haiti had traditional regimes in the period in question. As divided by *coups d'état,* there were four individual regimes, if a period of uncertainty in 1956–1957 is counted as one "regime." There was one radical-egalitarian regime in the period, the rebel regime occupying portions of Santo Domingo in the Dominican Republic from late April to early September, 1965. One regime, the popular revolutionary regime briefly in control of most of Hungary in 1956, has been classified as a citizen-community.

There were three independent totalitarian regimes at the beginning of the period (the U.S.S.R., Yugoslavia, and Albania). Five satellite regimes may be deemed independent by the end of the period (Bulgaria, Czechoslovakia, Hungary, Poland, and Romania). One regime was established by rebellion and victory in civil war in Cuba, the preceding regime which it replaced being trichotomized with a right. In these cases no *coups d'état* occurred. All nine regimes still existed at the end of the period. The same stability holds for representative-consensual regimes. There were twelve such regimes at the beginning and at the end of the period, all of which continued without interruption during the period (Australia, Canada, Denmark, Ireland, Mexico, the Netherlands, New Zealand, Norway, Sweden, Switzerland, the United Kingdom, and the United States). All were nonautocratic. Similarly, no *coups d'états* or other changes of regime in a continuing polity affected trichotomized regimes without a right in the period. There were five such regimes initially (Belgium, Costa Rica, Finland, Iceland, and Uruguay) and two (Austria and Japan) became independent during the period. All seven existed at the end of the period. All were nonautocratic.

For dichotomized regimes and trichotomized regimes with a right the situation is quite different. Most polities with such regimes showed considerable instability over the period. Only one dichotomized regime, the autocratic Somoza family dictatorship in Nicaragua, continued without interruption through the period. The other seven polities that initially had dichotomized regimes had successive regimes over the period as follows:

Bolivia (4 regimes)
1947–1951 nonautocratic
1951–1952 autocratic

1952–1964 autocratic
1964– autocratic

Dominican Republic (4 regimes)
1930–1962 autocratic
1962–1962 autocratic
1962–1963 nonautocratic
1963–1965 autocratic

El Salvador (2 regimes)
1948–1960 autocratic
1960– autocratic

Guatemala (3 regimes)
1944–1954 autocratic
1954–1963 autocratic
1963– autocratic

Honduras (4 regimes)
1933–1956 autocratic
1956–1958 autocratic
1958–1963 nonautocratic
1963– autocratic

Paraguay (3 regimes)
–1950 autocratic
1950–1954 autocratic
1954– autocratic

Peru (4 regimes)
1948–1956 autocratic
1956–1962 nonautocratic
1962–1963 autocratic
1963– autocratic.

Five trichotomized regimes with a right, two autocratic (Portugal and Spain) and three nonautocratic (Chile, Greece, and Italy), persisted throughout the period. As has been mentioned, one polity (Cuba) having a regime of this type was extinguished in civil war in 1958 and replaced by a polity with a totalitarian regime. There had been two regimes in the period in this case, a nonautocratic one ending in 1952, and an autocratic one lasting from 1952 to 1958. There was one other polity in this class (Panama) that had only two regimes during the period, one ending in 1951 and the other extending through the rest of the period, both autocratic. The other polities with trichotomized regimes with a right had three or more successive regimes in the period, as follows:

Argentina (4 regimes)
- 1930–1955 autocratic
- 1955–1958 autocratic
- 1958–1962 nonautocratic
- 1962– autocratic

Brazil (5 regimes)
- 1945–1951 autocratic
- 1951–1954 nonautocratic
- 1954–1955 autocratic
- 1955–1964 nonautocratic
- 1964– autocratic

Colombia (4 regimes)
- 1940–1953 nonautocratic
- 1953–1957 autocratic
- 1957–1958 autocratic
- 1958– nonautocratic

Ecuador (3 regimes)
- 1948–1961 nonautocratic
- 1961–1963 autocratic
- 1963– autocratic

France (3 regimes)
- 1945–1958 nonautocratic
- 1958–1959 autocratic
- 1959– nonautocratic

Venezuela (3 regimes)
1948–1958 autocratic
1958–1959 autocratic
1959– nonautocratic

SUMMARY

This chapter states the factual situation that the application to recent history of the new concepts of regime-types and of levels introduced in Chapters I and II respectively brings out. These factual observations may be stated in general terms as follows:

1. Consensual regimes (both the individual regimes and the type) are apparently totally stable "in a continuing polity" at all levels above Level 1.

2. Utopian regimes (both the individual regimes and the type) are apparently totally stable "in a continuing polity" at Levels 2 and 3. They have not been observed at Level 4.

3. Main-stem regimes take the dichotomized form at Level 2 and the trichotomized form, either with or without a right, at Level 3. At these levels the regime-types are exceedingly stable, but in most polities actual regimes (other than trichotomized regimes without a right, which are stable) are highly unstable. These regimes have not been observed at Level 4.

It will be the purpose of the next chapter to offer a theory tending to explain these observations.

CHAPTER IV

Stability and Change in Political Regimes—A Theory

CHAPTERS I and II introduced classificatory concepts for types of regimes and for socioeconomic levels. Chapter III used these concepts to organize an account of the political history of Western nation-states over the last three centuries or so. Analyzed in this way, the historical record shows certain striking regularities for which existing theories of politics offer no explanations. It is the purpose of the present chapter to advance a model (or way of thinking about the subject) and a theory (or set of formal assumptions) that tend to make the pattern of actual events brought out in Chapter II intelligible.

NECESSARY ELEMENTS FOR A THEORY

Theoretical explanation is the provision of a relatively simple set of ideas from which essential features of a complex body of actual phenomena may be deduced logically. Whereas, in Chapter III, types of regimes at different socioeconomic levels were described with some concreteness, it is now necessary to reason about this body of historical materials. In order to do so, attention must be concentrated upon selected abstract aspects of the regime-types and the levels rather than upon the full richness with which they appear in observation.[1]

The types of regimes will be regarded as states of the body of persons politically active in a given polity, a body of persons that may be referred to as the "leadership segment" of the polity. Similarly, the levels will be regarded as states of the whole body of persons belonging in some sense to the polity (systematically depressed ethnic castes or unassimilated tribal peoples being excluded in appropriate cases), a body of persons that may be referred to as the "population" of the polity. Distinctions among the populations occurring at the several levels and, for the most part, distinctions among the types of leadership segments in the several types of regimes will be treated as distinctions as to attitudes relevant to political action occurring within such populations and such leadership segments. If the four levels are viewed as four possible

[1]We are adopting a viewpoint stressed by some writers on the philosophy of science. We believe that the viewpoint that the entities of a theory are *merely* abstractions from observed phenomena (the viewpoint that implicitly underlies most reasoning in the social sciences) is heuristically unprofitable, at least in an area having the phenomenological richness of the historical record. We adopt instead the viewpoint that the entities in a theory are "postulated" or offered by an act of intellection or imagination and that a scientific theory differs from speculative philosophy *only* because the theoretical entities defined by postulates of the theory are conventionally linked with observable entities defined operationally. Thus, heat in modern physical theory is movement of molecules (in principle, postulated but unobservable), while heat in observation is (in everyday contexts) the length of a column of mercury in an evacuated tube. In the handling of observed phenomena we have been mainly influenced by the methodology of John Dewey and Arthur F. Bentley, *Knowing and the Known* (Boston, 1949), but in theory construction proper we have found more useful the methodology of F. S. C. Northrup in *The Logic of the Sciences and the Humanities* (New York, 1947).

attitudinal states of the population and the eight types of regimes are viewed as eight possible attitudinal states of the leadership segment of a polity, any theoretical explanation of the uniformities revealed in Chapter III must assign roles both to mass influences in politics and to the behavior of political elites.

If the theory is to be considered in relation to existing social and political theory, it needs to refer to less developed polities than those which occur, for the most part, in the narrative of Chapter III. A certain amount of theory—particularly in relation to democracy—has been formulated with reference to conditions in very simple societies. That such formulations can be generalized with regard to more advanced polities the present theory tends to deny. Hence, although Level 1 conditions—the citizen-community and traditional regimes—rarely occur in the political history of modern Western nation-states, the theory nevertheless briefly and in general terms extends to embrace them, if only to make distinctions between nonbureaucratic simple polities and bureaucratized polities occurring at the higher levels. Similarly, for completeness the theory makes reference to dependent polities, such as colonial possessions and countries under military occupation, even though these were largely overlooked in the empirical data collected in Chapter III.

Basically, the theory to be advanced must deal with the distinction between main-stem regimes at Level 2 and Level 3, and with the reasons for the stability of all regime-types (but especially of the consensual and utopian types) at these levels. Formally, the theory will deal with (1) statics—what regimes are viable at what levels—and (2) with dynamics only within a "continuing polity," that is, changes such as occur as the result of a promptly effective *coup d'état* or uprising, as well as peacefully or legally, but not charges coinciding with subjection to, or release from, dependent status as defined in Criterion 2. The theory does not attempt prognosis for organized warfare when two distinct regimes with territorial bases contend for control of the same territory, since special *ad hoc* considerations are likely to be decisive in such cases. Thus, the theory will imply, for instance, in reference to Cuba before the Castro victory, that a Communist take-over like that in Russia (in which previous social and political authority collapsed more or less simultaneously throughout the cities of Russia in November 1917) could not occur in Cuba, given the level attained, but the theory says nothing as to who will win if a crypto-Communist regime operating from a territorial base challenges militarily a reactionary dictatorship.

Finally, the ideas of the model that serve in the explanation of observed events at the lower levels allow the distinction of a Level 4 and suggest the nonviability of main-stem and totalitarian regimes at that level. This portion of the theory, however, since it extends beyond what existing data confirm, is relegated to the discussion of highly developed countries in Chapter VI.

POWER-WIELDING VIEWED AS STATUS-ASSERTION AND AS MANAGEMENT

In distinguishing attitudinal conditions characterizing populations at the several levels and leadership segments in the several types of regimes, a schematization as to possible viewpoints on the wielding of personal power will be used. This is an example of indirectly verifiable theory, since no attempt will be made to claim that evidence, such as survey responses, directly confirm what is postulated as to mass and elite attitudes. Rather, the argument is that if the attitudinal sets hereafter described are postulated, an explanation is offered for otherwise inexplicable regularities in phenomena. The cogency of the explanation and the lack of any equally simple rival explanation thus serve as a practical ground for belief in assumptions not themselves subjected to empirical confirmation. In the vew of many philosophers of science this seems to be the basic epistemological principle of modern science.

Abstractly considered, the wielding of power by persons over other persons may be viewed as either (1) the assertion of status, which may or may not be legitimate, or (2) as management, which may or may not serve the interests of a legitimate organization. Roughly, the first view is the way of perceiving power-wielding necessary for effective participation in a society largely composed of autonomics, while the second view is the way of perceiving power-wielding necessary for effective participation in a society dominated by large-scale organizations. The autonomic tends to view conspicuous exertions of power as, in essence, assertions of status on the part of the power-wielder, and any effective participant in a society lacking much large-scale organization must view power-wielding in this light much of the time. What may be called the "fully assimilated" member of the decision-audience, on the other hand, views power-wielding as the method by which those particular persons *who happen to have power* use that power rationally to control the actions of other persons, more or less powerful. That this latter "managerial" orientation to power-wielding expresses the logic of life within the decision-audience is obscured, especially at the lower levels of development, by the fact that most members of the decision-audience have too little obvious power over other persons to be much interested in its rational exercise. For the most part, until very high levels of development are reached, most members of the decision-audience retain the autonomic orientation toward power-wielding to a large extent. While this orientation is largely irrelevant to the day-by-day operations of any large-scale organization, it serves the purposes of general political life in societies not predominantly bureaucratized, and it also serves the purposes of joint assertions of power by groupings within large-scale organizations, most obviously in labor-management conflicts.

In order to make clear the abstract distinction between power-wielding viewed as management and viewed as the assertion of status, it is necessary to consider the possible ways in which power-wielding and management occur in the lives of members of both the autonomic component and of the decision-audience.[2]

An exertion of power consists of offers or threats (commonly implicit) likely to alter the motivations, and hence the conduct, of persons other than the power-wielder. It may occur within an intimate group—a family or family-like structure—(both the power-wielder and those affected being participants in the group), or it may occur outside such a group (the power-wielder not being a full participant in any intimate group to which all those affected by the exertion of power belong). In the former case the exertion of power is likely to be determined by, and in any case will be more

[2]We are introducing in this section the elements of what is called a "model" as distinguished from a "theory" by certain methodologists, e.g., Ernest Nagel, *The Structure of Science* (New York, 1961), and R. B. Braithwaite, *Scientific Explanation* (Cambridge, 1955). In this usage a "model" is a way of thinking in terms meaningful to the imagination that facilitates reasoning about relationships reflected in certain phenomena. In this usage the "theory" proper is only those formal logical relationships embedded in the model that are reflected in the observed relationships among phenomena. Sometimes theorizing successfully goes beyond any plausible model, as in modern quantum physics, which is mathematically consistent as abstract theory and is explicative of phenomena but in which the explicative relationships cannot be imagined in terms of any one consistent model.

or less masked by appeals to, internalized norms shared by all participants in the group. Power-wielding in such a context performs no obvious function independent of the shared normative system possessed by the intimate group. It is only with the exertion of power outside this context that the present argument is concerned.

Exertions of power outside intimate groups operate in one of two normally distinct ways: the assertion of status or management. An exertion of power that asserts status tends to establish the ability of a person or grouping of persons to act within certain limits and at the same time to establish the inability of other persons to act in ways inconsistent with the power of action so asserted. The characteristic of an exertion of power that asserts status thus lies in the generality of its effects. It presumes that persons affected will continue to act autonomously within established limits rather than to act in response to current directions. It tends to maintain or to restrict the limits on their actions. Such an exertion of power may appear as a private act in the interest of the power-wielder or of his associates, or it may appear to be a disinterested determination of the rights of parties other than the power-wielder, as in adjudication or legislation. An exertion of power in the nature of management, on the other hand, tends to determine a particular action or course of action by a specific person or by specific persons. The context to which it relates is specific and current, and it has few obvious generalized implications for future conduct outside this specific current context.

To be recognized as managerial, an exertion of power must be seen as affecting a type of activity that could not be carried on without authoritative decision-making. Otherwise, it will be perceived in terms of its general implications as to status and will be regarded as an act asserting status. Thus, the same exertion of power may be an assertion of status from the standpoint of those affected by it and an act of management from the standpoint of the power-wielder and sometimes vice versa.

The activities normally carried on by members of the autonomic component are not, at least from their point of view, subject to management. The operations carried on within a family-type farm or artisan enterprise are largely determined by internalized norms shared by participants, and (as long as some minimal input of resources and output of products in exchange occurs) they will go on without the interposition of outside authority. The purely internal activities of such a group appear to occur autonomously, and those activities of the group which involve outsiders appear similarly to occur autonomously but within limits determined by the accepted statuses of the persons involved. It is often a matter of status to be able to engage in certain occupations at all. It is usually a matter of status to what extent contributions of product, or its money equivalent, must pass out of the group in the form of taxes, rent, or tribute. In the life of the autonomic, therefore, there is little legitimate role for the deliberate use of power managerially, that is, to cause persons to do or not to do specific acts for other purposes than the symbolic assertion of status.

While it is only a member of the autonomic component who can with much real consistency reject management (as it affects him) as a legitimate use of power, the characteristic attitude of the autonomic can readily be adopted by other persons in the assertion of their desired statuses. Those who manage large enterprises often take the characteristic autonomic attitude with respect to power coming from outside their organizations if they can plausibly claim a status of independence. Thus, large business organizations (within which the exercise of managerial power is normal and pervasive) commonly treat exertions of external power as asserting status rather than as managerial. Similarly, independent professionals (although their own activities largely involve the manipulation of the wills of persons not linked with them in intimate groups) may also adopt toward outside regulation the characteristic attitude of the autonomic.

Contexts calling for management nevertheless occur to some extent even among autonomics. A company of persons assembled for fighting cannot operate effectively unless under some form of personal command. The casual co-operation of several persons in manual labor, as in raising the frame of a building, requires that someone give the cues for the joint exertion of muscular power. Where the state of technology requires the co-operation of a certain number of people in such a task as hunting or fishing, it is useless for participants to make their own decisions individually as to what trail to pursue or what waters to seine. The minimum number of persons must act together or not at all. While management of a sort is necessary to such activities as these when engaged in casually by persons whose normal activities place them within the autonomic component, no serious exertion of power is normally involved. In activities of the sort mentioned, leadership normally arises casually and leaders in special activities do not necessarily wield much *power* in these or in other activities. The autonomic, therefore, unless occasionally drafted into forced labor or military service, has no experience with the serious exertion of *power* in contexts he might recognize as legitimately managerial.

All activities not carried on by autonomics in families or family-like structures or entered into casually and temporarily under leaders accepted for the occasion occur in what may be called "bureaucratic" organizations (in a very broad sense of the term). In these organizations many current decisions within the work process cannot be made rationally except on the basis of prior decisions of more or less remote persons. This is merely to say that an appearance of autonomous decision-making by persons working together can occur only when a distinct small working group shares a sufficient body of relevant internalized norms. In some sorts of activities and in all large organizations no adequate single set of such norms could possibly develop. If these activities are of a casual or emergency nature, they may be engaged in by autonomics either spontaneously or by virtue of an established status obligation, as in the case of militia service. When such activities go on continuously, the participants become members of the decision-audience.

It is the characteristic of members of the decision-audience that they are engaged fairly permanently in activities within bureaucratic organizations. While particular working groups within such an organization often develop fairly uniform internalized norms, these are irrelevant to many needs of the organization as a whole and can not cover current decision-making as completely as in a family-like structure of autonomics. While leadership in many casual activities performed by autonomics is casually chosen and is exercised without the exertion of serious power, the managerial function is always somewhat specialized and involves power-wielding at every level of bureaucratic organization. Even if persons are promoted from the ranks, they are rarely demoted. The decision-maker at every level of organization usually has attained a permanent status higher than that of his subordinates. From the permanence of his functional assignment alone, if from no other circumstance, he derives substantial power over those subordinate to his formal powers of decision-making.

It is necessary for power (and hence some permanence of status) to be generally associated with the function of decision-making within bureaucratic organizations, because there is always a conflict of interest between the responsible decision-maker and subordinate operating personnel. This is true even if the obvious interest of the worker in avoiding excessively burdensome working conditions is ignored. In the best state of morale, operating personnel are oriented to the performance of their specialized tasks in the most technically efficient way possible. Such performance is rarely compatible with the allocation of resources determined at higher levels within the organization and may, especially in the case of a regulatory organization, be incompatible with the effective power of the organization in the face of outside power. In any complex organization, management mainly involves the restraint of those over whom the manager has effective power in the interest of the meshing of their activities with those of outside categories over which he lacks similar power. While he may press upon superiors views consonant with those of his subordinates, he always comes back from such contacts with the need to enforce limitations upon the attainment of the needs, goals, and standards of his subordinates. Thus, in a bureaucratic context management is rarely leadership. It is usually restraint and control. Leadership, in the sense of innovation consonant with the standards of participants, usually occurs at every level of organization among formal subordinates. Its proposals are accepted, rejected, or modified by the responsible decision-maker acting under considerations somewhat remote from those motivating his subordinates.

Because what is here called the orientation that sees power-wielding as asserting status has long pervaded conscious political thinking of all ideological shades, it is necessary to stress that what is here called the managerial orientation is a totally different way of looking at power-wielding and is not equivalent to the attitude of those who assert high status for some category of persons who might be called "managers." The status orientation toward power-wielding does not see power-wielding as a continuous aspect of life. It looks only to the *possibilities* that persons may exert power over other persons. It judges actual or imagined exertions of power to be legitimate only as they assert statuses judged to be legitimate. It does not see the power of persons over other persons as necessarily existing in one contingent form or another without any strict conformance to standards that may be believed in as to who ought and who ought not to have power. The managerial viewpoint, on the contrary, takes the contingent power of persons over other persons as given in all social contexts. It envisages only contexts permeated by actually exerted, not merely potential, power. It judges those exertions of power legitimate that contingently serve the purposes of a legitimate organization—and, in principle, regardless of whose particular status they inflate or deflate.

It is only the status orientation toward power-wielding that supports the ideological judgments historically characteristic of political movements and causes. The status orientation admits conceptually of many different ideal standards for the status-order. It is compatible with strict egalitarianism (only one legitimate category of persons being recognized) and with various forms and degrees of defined inequalitarianism. It admits of various ordered views of the ideal society. It is only incompatible with, or meaningless with relation to, the kind of total intermeshing of contingent personal powers, great and small, which occurs in very highly organized social contexts. The managerial orientation, on the other hand, can admit neither strict egalitarianism nor reliably fixed social stratifications as meaningful norms in real life. It takes for granted that different persons will have unequal power in every context where action is called for and that the action taken will reflect this contingent arrangement of personal powers and not some other imaginary distribution of powers that might be judged in some sense preferable. It assumes that persons who happen to possess power in any given situation will use the power they possess in ways that will modify its distribution among persons in the future.

Management (abstractly considered) sees the exertion of individual power as occurring within organizational contexts which its exercise preserves, destroys, or modifies. While in form it commonly judges an exercise of power according to purposes that the organization is supposed to serve in the larger society, at the higher levels of managerial power such a criterion can seldom be applied in practical decision-making except by translating it into the criterion of organizational survival. Standards, goals, and interests of relatively subordinate participants give any large organization its functional purposes and its motivations for action. These purposes and motivations need not and cannot be provided by the wielding of managerial power. Thus, to a limited degree, the participants in a bureaucratic organization act autonomously under internalized norms as do the participants in an autonomic enterprise, but only to a limited degree. A bureaucratic organization is never capable of directly supplying the basic needs of its members (as is, for instance, a subsistence farm) nor is it related to the larger society only by relatively simple exchanges of commodities (as are most autonomic enterprises). It lives by virtue of the inflow of resources that other bureaucratic organizations or bodies of autonomic producers supply, and it exerts power by virtue of the support or tolerance of similar external entities. It is the function of higher management to see that activities internal to the organization mesh with each other and with outside activities in such a way that the organization can continue to exist. Unlike the leadership of autonomic structures, management in a bureaucratic organization can perform its function only by obviously limiting the impulse of subordinates to follow internalized norms.

Because of the ambiguous relation of managerial power-wielding to the interests, goals, and standards of subordinates, the mere fact that it pervades and limits all activities within bureaucratic organizations does not lead to the full acceptance of management as a legitimate form of power-wielding by all participants in such organizations. In general, only those who manage can readily understand and accept the rationale under which management operates. The manual decision-audience is normally hostile toward managerial activities. So, quite commonly, are specialized white-collar operating personnel who themselves exercise no serious managerial power over subordinates. To both these groupings, while the autonomic orientation remains prevalent within the polity in which they live, this orientation remains congenial even if strictly irrelevant to most of their day-to-day activities. They prefer to think of legitimate power-wielding as the assertion of suitable statuses within which persons may autonomously perform their several activities. Therefore, only a portion of the nonmanual decision-audience readily adopts the managerial orientation as its own.

There are thus two basic orientations toward power that tend to prevail within a population:

1. The status orientation characteristic of the autonomic component and widely held in other portions of the population except at the highest levels is: "Persons properly act autonomously within and only within the limits set by their legitimate statuses."

2. The managerial orientation, widely held within more or less managerial portions of the nonmanual decision-audience is: "Persons properly act autonomously within and only within the limits set by current decisions of persons exercising authority over their activities in the interests of organizational survival."

As has been pointed out, the managerial orientation toward power-wielding does not support ideological distinctions. Techniques for using such personal power as one may possess within a highly organized context take account only of the organization as a whole (and the possibility of its definition in larger or smaller terms) and of the contingent personal powers actually existing within it. They cannot be usefully employed in support of imaginary standards of where power should be. The case is entirely different with the status orientation toward power-wielding. This orientation is readily modified according to idealized standards as to what statuses are or are not proper and, in fact, without such a standard being embodied within it, it is a meaningless guide to action. In practice the status orientation to power-wielding tends to break down into two abstract viewpoints as to the legitimacy of statuses. When policy is viewed under the status orientation, every person in every very specific context appears to act under one or the other of two abstract suborientations: (1) the rightist orientation, "The proper statuses of persons are the statuses they currently enjoy;" and (2) the leftist orientation, "The proper statuses of persons are those demonstrably appropriate to the functions they currently need to perform." In a very specific context, everyone who challenges the *status quo* takes the leftist orientation, and everyone who supports the *status quo* (either in principle or because the work of existing organizations must go on) takes the rightist orientation. Thus considered, these attitudes are strictly relative to a particular situation. Neither can be adopted rationally for all contexts of daily life. No one can consistently be a rightist and accept every organizational situation that presents itself. No one can consistently be a leftist, since this orientation leaves all organization in flux while its suitability to a current and ever-vanishing situation is under appraisal. Thus, in a situation where one bears responsibility for action, no one can be consistently a leftist or a rightist. Such a person is inevitably drawn away from a status orientation toward a managerial orientation.

The case is otherwise for persons who bear no clear responsibility for the outcome of current developments. While they hold the general status orientation toward power-wielding, they readily become leftists or rightists in relation to the broader current issues of public policy. In respect to their own relations with outside authorities and higher social strata, the members of the autonomic component are always leftist in orientation. When, as is true at Levels 1 and 2, the autonomics regard themselves simply as the "common people," this means that the prevailing popular attitude is necessarily leftist. The members of the manual decision-audience, because of their lack of involvement in serious decision-making, likewise adopt the leftist orientation. While this component remains small, as it does at Level 2, it is hardly distinguishable in culture from the autonomic component and forms with that component a numerically dominant leftist "common people" or "mechanic class." Once the manual decision-audience is larger and forms a self-perpetuating social formation, as it does when Level 3 is reached, it becomes clearly differentiated culturally from the autonomic component. The interest of the latter lies deeply in the forms of private property that tend to support their autonomy from outside control. Private property has no serious functional meaning in the lives of the members of the manual decision-audience, and the attitude of members of this component is hostile (with various degrees of ideological rationalization) to the claims of status which reflect property rights. With the full differentiation of the manual decision-audience, the autonomic component no longer sees itself simply as the "common people." Rather, it sees its acquired status as appreciably threatened by the self-assertions of the manual decision-audience. Thus, the attitude of the autonomic component becomes a mélange of the leftist orientation in relation to social superiors and the rightist orientation in relation to social inferiors. Once this change has occurred, the leftist orientation can no longer be said to be the prevailing popular attitude, since the consistently leftist manual decision-audience always remains a minority.

A THEORETICAL MEANING FOR THE LEVELS

In the preceding section, possible orientations toward power-wielding were classified as managerial or status, and the latter was further classified as rightist or leftist. These ideas allow the assignment of distinct theoretical meanings to the four levels of development. To state these meanings, three simple (as distinguished from compound) statements suffice. It will be convenient to have abbreviations for such basic theoretical statements. The form for such abbreviations will be a small letter followed by a capital letter. The abbreviations for the three statements characterizing the levels will be distinguished by including small *p,* since they all refer to the state of a population. These three statements and their abbreviations are the following:

pM—The managerial orientation occurs significantly within the population, at least as a private orientation of influential persons.

pS—The status orientation to power-wielding prevails within the population.

pL—The leftist orientation toward power-wielding prevails within the population.

The managerial orientation cannot be a significant orientation unless there are large-scale organizations to the management of which powerful persons may devote most of their time and attention. It can hardly be other than a significant orientation, at least privately among influential persons, when such organizations exist. Thus, *pM* may be taken to refer to the condition prevailing at all levels except Level 1.

(1) The theoretical statement *pM* will be deemed to be equivalent to the observational statement that a polity is at a level other than Level 1.[3]

The status orientation, rather than the managerial orien-

[3]As the form of this statement indicates, we do not intend to offer systematic evidence tending to demonstrate directly that *pM* is true in and only in polities at levels above Level 1. The theory we offer is an indirectly verifiable theory. By such assumptions as this one we give theoretical meanings to the observed levels and the observed regime-types. We then offer a set of hypotheses, expressed in the theoretical rather than the observational language, and show that this set of hypotheses determines logically the occurrence and changes of regimes in relation to levels in the same way in which they are actually observed to occur. In the methodological viewpoint here adopted (see note 1 above), successful theorizing in the exact sciences is seen as analyzable into this form of thinking. A statement linking a theoretical with an observable concept as in some sense "the same thing," like the numbered statements in this and the following section of our exposition, is called an "epistemic correlation" by Northrup, *op. cit.*, ch. vii, and perhaps more commonly a "coordinating definition" by other methodologists. This general type of thought-form is discussed at length under the heading "Rules of Correspondence" by Nagel, *op. cit.*, pp. 97–105.

tation, has obviously been the prevailing one in historical societies. The so-called "end of ideology" in countries of highly advanced economic structure, recently commented upon,[4] could clearly be a consequence of a diminishing hold of the status orientation upon the populations of such countries under the argument previously advanced. The historical prevalence of the status orientation should be terminated once the nonmanual decision-audience (always significantly influenced by the managerial orientation) becomes so large as necessarily to be widely linked by family relationships with members of the other working-force components. This would seem to be the case when the nonmanual decision-audience reaches 40 per cent of the working force.[5] Level 4 may thus be regarded as the condition in which *pS* is not true.

(2) The theoretical statement *pS* will be deemed to be equivalent to the observational statement that a polity is at a level other than Level 4.

It has been noted that the leftist orientation is the prevailing one while the autonomic component, which tends to hold this orientation, can view itself as equivalent to the "common people"; however, this leftist orientation is no longer the prevailing one once the manual decision-audience is numerous and clearly distinguished culturally from the autonomic component. Since this differentiation of the manual decision-audience is the mark of the attainment of Level 3, Levels 1 and 2 together may be regarded as the condition in which *pL* is true.

[4]Daniel Bell, *The End of Ideology; On the Exhaustion of Political Ideas in the Fifties* (New York, 1961).

[5]Seymour Lipset, *Social Mobility in Industrial Society* (Berkeley and Los Angeles, 1960), ch. i, collects a variety of studies tending to show a fairly constant rate of social mobility of 20 per cent to 30 per cent as between white collar and manual employment in industrialized societies.

(3) The theoretical statement pL will be deemed to be equivalent to the observational statement that a polity is either at Level 1 or at Level 2.

These three statements together characterize each of the four levels by a unique combination of the truth values of the statements pM, pS, and pL. The theoretical meaning assigned to the levels is shown in Diagram 2.

Diagram 2. Theoretical correlates of observed levels

Level 1	Level 2	Level 3	Level 4
not pM	pM		
pS			not pS
pL		not pL	

Thus, Level 1 is the condition in which pM is not true but both of pS and pL are true; Level 2 is the condition in which pM, pS, and pL are all true; Level 3 is the condition in which pM and pS are both true and pL is not true; and Level 4 is the condition in which pM is true but neither pS nor pL is true. There can logically be no condition in which pL is true while pS is not true, since the leftist orientation is a variant of the status orientation. There is no empirical level that could be identified with a condition in which neither pM nor pL is true, since pM is true at all levels other than Level 1, and here pL is true.

It will be noted that the theoretical representation of the levels does not include intervening stages such as are recognized in empirical report. The intention is that a theoretical statement that something occurs at a particular level will be confirmed by an empirical finding of that level or of either adjacent intervening range. This raises the question of whether the interlevel ranges are real or are merely practical concessions to the possible inaccuracy or noncomparability of data from which level is determined empirically. The question is left open since it is not vital to the argument presented. If the intervening ranges are real, the theory is, of course, oversimplified, but this is a convenient characteristic of much useful theory.

A THEORETICAL MEANING FOR THE REGIME-TYPES

The possible orientations toward power-wielding as characterized in an earlier section can be used in giving theoretical meanings to the regime-types as well as to the levels. For this purpose three simple statements will suffice. Since the statements relating to regime-types all refer to the condition of a leadership segment, they will be distinguished by including small *s* in their abbreviations. The three statements and abbreviations are the following:

sM—The orientation of the leadership segment toward politics is managerial.

sL—An important portion of the leadership segment consistently views politics with a leftist orientation.

sR—An important portion of the leadership segment consistently views politics with a rightist orientation.

Certain other ideas will, however, be necessary to distinguish all the regime-types. There is, first, the distinction between the condition in very simple societies where persons exercise political leadership largely on a part-time or amateur basis and spend most of their time either in other occupations or in leisured activities and the condition in more developed societies where, for the most part, political leadership is a full-time pursuit (whether or not formally compensated or treated as an occupational status). There is also a necessary distinction between a leadership segment in a dependent polity, which is essentially a subordinate appendage of the leadership segment of another polity, and a leadership segment in a substantially independent polity. Finally, the situation must be recognized where a leadership segment conceives of itself, as in a totalitarian regime, as performing an essentially tutelary role because its effective membership consists of persons fully instructed in some officially promulgated, construed, and propagated doctrine, conformance with which is considered essential for the proper development of the polity. The following statements will serve to make these distinctions:

sF—The leadership segment consists of persons who devote their whole time to political activities (broadly construed).

sO—The leadership segment is a subordinate appendage to that of another polity.

sT—The leadership segment is a body of persons who view their role as tutelary with respect to the exposition and enforcement of an official ideology.

The theoretical distinction between *sF* and not-*sF* is intended to be the same as the empirical distinction between the nonapplicability and the applicability of Criterion 3.

(1) The theoretical statement *sF* will be deemed to be equivalent to the observational statement that the regime is neither citizen-community, nor traditional, nor radical-egalitarian.

The condition indicated by the statement *sO* is intended to be the same as the empirical condition indicated by the applicability of Criterion 2.

(2) The theoretical statement *sO* will be deemed to be equivalent to the observational statement that the polity is dependent.

The tutelary character of a leadership segment indicated by the statement *sT* may be regarded as the condition prevailing in a utopian regime with a full-time leadership segment, that is, in a regime to which Criterion 1 applies but to which Criterion 3 does not apply.

(3) The theoretical statement *sT* will be regarded as equivalent to the observational statement that the regime is totalitarian.

As characterized in an earlier section, the managerial orientation toward power-wielding tends to lead to decision-making governed primarily by the needs for organizational survival. If the leadership segment of a regime is managerial in orientation, as is indicated by the statement *sM*, it should succeed in preserving the regime except in situations involving the intrusion of overwhelming outside-based power (situations that are outside the universe of discourse set for the formal theory), and it should be able to do so without permitting serious public disorders to recur regularly. Thus, *sM* may be identified with the regime-types whose individual regimes are stable and in which public disorders are not anticipated as a normal thing, that is, for regimes above Level 1, with representative-consensual or totalitarian regimes. The statement *sM* cannot be associated with the citizen-community regime, since the part-time leadership segment drawn from the general population at Level 1 could not be managerial in orientation.

(4) The theoretical statement *sM* will be deemed to be equivalent to the observational statement that the regime is either representative-consensual or totalitarian.

The presence of an imporant rightist element in the leadership segment may be identified with what is called in the discussion of empirical regimes either a traditionalist-personalist right or a *de facto* right. It will be recalled that the presence of one or the other of these entities is indicated by the applicability of Criterion 2, 4, or 5 and is the condition common to all main-stem regime-types except the trichotomized regime without a right.

(5) The theoretical statement *sR* will be deemed to be equivalent to the observational statement that the regime-type is traditional, dichotomized, trichotomized with a right, dependent dichotomized, or dependent trichotomized.

In the empirical criteria, the dichotomized regime is characterized by the presence of an influential generalized left tending to embrace all rationalist-institutionalist tendencies. Such a left is present in an incipient form in that portion of the common people that tends to carry on localized administration in a traditional regime. A radicalized residue of such a left carries over as the dominant tendency in a radical-egalitarian regime. The left referred to in the statement *sL* may be identified with these various empirical manifestations of a left. It cannot be identified with portions of the leadership segment in other regime-types. Once transformed into a tutelary ruling party in a totalitarian regime, a radical elite of leftist origin can hardly be strictly leftist any longer in the sense of being critically skeptical of existing institutional arrangements. In trichotomized regimes the old generalized left has broken up. The highly egalitarian tendency which tends to pre-empt the term "left" in these regimes is not very effectively admitted to the leadership segment. What else remains of the old left is not very consistently leftist.

(6) The theoretical statement *sL* will be deemed equivalent to the observational statement that the regime is traditional, radical-egalitarian, or dichotomized.

If the condition "not-*sO*" is assumed, i.e., that the polity is not dependent, the foregoing six statements associate each of the eight observable independent regime-types with a unique combination of the truth values of *sM*, *sR*, *sL*, *sF*, and *sT* as is shown in Diagram 3.

Diagram 3. Theoretical correlates of observed independent regime-types

<table>
<tr><td rowspan="8">not sO</td><td rowspan="3">not sF</td><td rowspan="2">not sR</td><td>not sL</td><td rowspan="6">not sM</td><td rowspan="7">not sT</td><td>Citizen-Community</td></tr>
<tr><td rowspan="3">sL</td><td>Radical-egalitarian</td></tr>
<tr><td rowspan="3">sR</td><td>Traditional</td></tr>
<tr><td rowspan="5">sF</td><td>Dichotomized</td></tr>
<tr><td rowspan="4">not sL</td><td>Trichotomized with right</td></tr>
<tr><td rowspan="3">not sR</td><td>Trichotomized without right</td></tr>
<tr><td rowspan="2">sM</td><td>Representative-consensual</td></tr>
<tr><td>sT</td><td>Totalitarian</td></tr>
</table>

In drafting the criteria that distinguish regime-types empirically, certain assumptions regarding dependent regimes were made a matter of definition. It was assumed that in a nontotalitarian regime the representatives of foreign power function politically as a right and hence that any dependent nontotalitarian regime is necessarily of main-stem type. It was also assumed that no dependent regime could, strictly speaking, have the full characteristics of either a traditional or a radical-egalitarian regime and that dependent regimes approximating these forms could best be regarded as dichotomized or totalitarian regimes respectively. If these definitional aspects of the concepts by which observations are reported are to be reflected in the theoretical concepts (as they must be), it must be assumed that *sO* implies *sF* and either *sR* or *sT*. With the addition of this assumption, the six statements given above associate each observable dependent regime-type with a unique combination of the truth values of *sM, sR, sL, sF,* and *sT* as in Diagram 4.

Diagram 4. Theoretical correlates of observed dependent regime-types

<table>
<tr><td rowspan="3">sO</td><td rowspan="3">sF</td><td rowspan="2">sR</td><td>sL</td><td rowspan="2">not sM</td><td rowspan="2">not sT</td><td>Dependent dichotomized</td></tr>
<tr><td rowspan="2">not sL</td><td>Dependent trichotomized</td></tr>
<tr><td>not sR</td><td>sM</td><td>sT</td><td>Dependent totalitarian</td></tr>
</table>

THEORY I. STATICS: RESTRICTIONS ON THE STATE OF THE LEADERSHIP SEGMENT BY THE STATE OF THE GENERAL POPULATION

The present section deals with the viability of the several regime-types at the several levels. The static theory expresses relations between the condition of a leadership segment—indicated by statements *sM, sR, sL, sF, sO,* and *sT*—and the condition of the general population—indicated by statements *pM, pS,* and *pL.*

Evidently the condition of a population indicated by *pM* is both a necessary and a sufficient condition for the kind of leadership segment indicated by *sF.* If there are some bureaucratic organizations within a polity to whose management some power-wielders must devote substantially their full time and attention (as is indicated by *pM*), then all important power-wielders, including especially the political elite or leadership segment, will have to be involved in power-wielding on essentially a full-time basis. Conversely, if the leadership segment itself has a full-time character, as would be true if there are significant governmental bureaucracies, then the condition indicated by *pM* is necessarily satisfied for the population as a whole. To express these and other theoretical statements formally, a notation using the period (.) for conjunction ("and"), V for disjunction ("or" as in "either A or B or both"), and the overline ($\overline{X}$) for negation will be used. (Two terms immediately joined by the period are assumed to go together in preference to two terms joined by V unless parentheses are used to change this presumption.) Thus, the foregoing relation between *pM* and *sF* may be summarily stated as follows:

Hypothesis 1: *pM* is equivalent to *sF*[6]

On the basis of the associations previously established between theoretical and observational terms, Hypothesis 1 carries the following meaning in observational terms:

(1) At levels above Level 1 (that is, when *pM* is true), only the following regime-types (those for which *sF* is true) occur: dichotomized, trichotomized with right, trichotomized without right, representative-consensual, totalitarian.

(2) At Level 1 (that is, when *pM* is not true), only the following regime-types (those for which *sF* is not true) occur: citizen-community, traditional, radical-egalitarian.

Chapter III assembles rather generous evidence tending to

[6]In logic, to say that two statements are "equivalent" means that when one is true the other is true and when one is false the other is false. In other words, each of the two statements implies the other.

confirm the first of these verifiable consequences of Hypothesis 1. The limitation of evidence to modern Western nation-states precluded the systematic accumulation of evidence relevant to the second of these verifiable consequences, but both anthropological studies and histories of the ancient and medieval periods tend to confirm the expectation that in very simple societies political regimes tend to conform to the citizen-community or traditional types rather than to others in the classificatory scheme here used.

As far as the radical-egalitarian type of regime is concerned, given its ephemeral and somewhat disorganized character, there is no way of directly confirming empirically that it occurs at Level 1. Tabulations of reliable data normally relate to earlier or later times in the same polity. Moreover, in all probability occupational and status distributions would not be greatly altered in form during a radical-egalitarian regime so that even a census taken at the time of such a regime might not directly confirm the general weakening of bureaucratic organization on which the Level 1 assignment of this regime-type is theoretically based. It may be that the placing of this regime-type at Level 1 is merely a convenient way of representing it in terms of the model. If so, it seems to lie within the license available to the model-builder, because it does not confuse any actual processes of empirical observation.

Hypothesis 1 must be treated as irrevalent for a dependent polity. In such a case, pM is presumed to hold because of the military and bureaucratic personnel supported from outside the polity in order to maintain its dependent status, regardless of what an occupational census of the local population might show as to level.

A full-time leadership segment necessarily consists of persons who belong to the nonmanual decision-audience. It has been pointed out that leftist attitudes naturally develop consistently and spontaneously only within the manual decision-audience and the autonomic component. A significant leftist orientation within a full-time leadership segment would therefore occur only as a reflection of the prevalence of this attitude within the population.

Hypothesis 2: $sF.sL$ implies pL.

Since sF and sL are both true only for a dichotomized regime and since pL is true only for Levels 1 and 2, the observable meaning of Hypothesis 2 is that a dichotomized regime does not occur at levels above Level 2. This is rather adequately validated by the data in Chapter III.

When the prevailing orientation in the population is leftist and the leadership segment has a full-time character, the searchings by various less secure members of the leadership segment for support will maintain a left within the leadership segment unless this segment has a managerial orientation.

Hypothesis 3: $pL.sF.\overline{sM}$ implies sL.

This means in observational terms that a main-stem regime at Level 2 must be dichotomized, that is, that it cannot be trichotomized either with or without a right. This is also rather adequately confirmed by the data in Chapter III.

Aside from some less certain propositions setting off Level 4 (to be presented in Chapter VI), Hypotheses 1, 2, and 3 establish the statics of the theory. In theoretical terms, they set up the relationships between states of the general population and states of the leadership segment shown in Diagram 5.

Thus, where the prevailing popular attitude is leftist but there is no significant bureaucratic organization (Level 1), only a nonbureaucratized form of leadership segment (i.e.,

Diagram 5. Summary of static theory

	Level 1	Level 2	Levels 3 and 4
States of population	$\overline{pM}\cdot pL$	$pM\cdot pL$	$pM\cdot\overline{pL}$
Consequent limitations on states of leadership segments	$\overline{sF}$	$sF\cdot(sL \vee sM)$	$sF\cdot\overline{sL}$

one whose participants do not devote full time to this activity) is viable. Where there is significant bureaucratic organization (all levels but Level 1), only a bureaucratized leadership segment (i.e., one whose participants devote full time to this activity) is viable. If besides significant bureaucratic organization there is also a prevailing leftist attitude in the population (Level 2), then the leadership segment must either be managerial in orientation or contain a significant left within itself. If besides significant bureaucratic organization there is not a prevailing leftist attitude in the population (Levels 3 and 4), the leadership segment cannot contain a significant left within itself.

In the terms in which observations are reported, therefore, the static theory states that (1) only citizen-community, traditional, and radical-egalitarian regimes occur at Level 1; (2) only representative-consensual, dichotomized, and totalitarian regimes occur at Level 2; and (3) only representative-consensual, trichotomized without a right, trichotomized with a right, and totalitarian regimes occur at levels above Level 2.

REGIMES IN NEWLY FORMED POLITIES

Since the formal dynamic theory, to be stated in the next section, refers only to events in a continuing polity, only the static theory limits what regimes may occur initially in new polities. Although *ad hoc* considerations play a large role in the origin and also in the termination of polities and hence generalization is difficult, it may clarify the practical significance of the model and theory if the commoner ways in which different regime-types occur in newly formed polities are enumerated.

Since the classification "citizen-community" in the present scheme includes the simpler forms of tribal organization of nonliterate peoples, this regime-type must have originated most commonly, historically, from the migration of a small band of persons of more or less equal status and their subsequent settlement in vacant land (or land from which they had driven previous occupants). It could also be formed by rebellion driving out, or exterminating, leisured aristocrats in what was previously a polity with a traditional regime. Traditional regimes must normally have been created by the conquest of a territorial area, already populated, by a mobile band of fighting men, perhaps advantaged by the possession of horses or superior weapons, and their settling themselves in their conquest as a dominant class among the previous inhabitants.

Although sometimes formed by the sudden transformation of an existing polity, as will be treated under the dynamic theory in the next section, a radical-egalitarian regime may also be created locally by rebellion. Since it presumes, in many respects, cultural features of levels higher than Level 1, such a rebellion probably occurs only within territory previously at one of the higher levels.

Aside from the three Level 1 polities, the origins of regimes in new polities probably have occurred most commonly in recent times by subjection to, or release from, dependency status.

Subjection of an area to dependent status at Level 1 or Level 2 creates a dependent dichotomized regime, and at Level 3 or Level 4 creates a dependent trichotomized regime. Possibly, in either case, the regime initially created could also be dependent totalitarian, but more likely this would be created by a later transformation, as was the case with the various Russian satellite polities in Eastern Europe after World War II.

Liberation of a territory at Level 1 from dependent status would necessarily create one or more polities with either citizen-community or traditional regimes, the latter depending on the circumstance that a leisured aristocratic class was left in effective dominance of a region.

Liberation of a polity at Level 2 would normally transform a dependent totalitarian into an independent totalitarian regime or a dependent dichotomized into an independent dichotomized regime. However, experience indicates that if several conditions are met, what has been a dependent dichotomized regime may become representative-consensual at liberation. This probably happened in most of the original United States at the time of the Revolution and possibly in some of the Dutch provinces at the time of the rebellion against Spain. The essential condition seems to be that the native elite should see itself at the moment of liberation as an essentially homogeneous interest united in opposition to the retiring "right" representing the former foreign rulers. Other conditions would presumably be necessary to avoid such confusions in the new polity as would immediately produce raw confrontations of force and thus perpetuate the expectation of internal basic conflict that determines mainstem regimes. Some degree of experience with representative politics on the part of the native elite before liberation would appear to be necessary, as would the opportunity to continue or to create an initial set of recognized governing institutions. Also, it would appear to be necessary that the local leadership be agreed upon just what territory (or territories) was being transformed into an independent polity or into independent polities. It will be noted that all these conditions were unsatisfied in the Spanish American colonies at the time of their liberation.

Liberation from foreign rule at a level higher than Level 2 would presumably transform a dependent totalitarian regime into an independent totalitarian regime and could transform, according to circumstances, a dependent trichotomized regime into a trichotomized regime with a right, a trichotomized regime without a right, or a representative-consensual regime. The latter outcome would probably depend upon satisfying the same set of conditions as at Level 2. If the essential condition for a representative-consensual regime—the conscious unity of the native elite—is not satisfied but the other conditions are and, in addition, no institutional base is left for a "right," whether traditionalist-personalist or *de facto,* then the resulting regime will apparently be trichotomized without a right, as in the case of Japan after the occupation following World War II.

If it is true, as is proposed in Chapter VI, that no regime is viable in an independent polity at Level 4 except a representative-consensual regime, then liberation at that level would presumably transform either a dependent totalitarian or a dependent trichotomized regime into a representative-consensual regime.

THEORY II. DYNAMICS: LIMITATIONS ON REGIME CHANGES IN A CONTINUING POLITY

Assumption 1. Since a regime change coinciding with subjection to, or release from, dependent status is conventionally treated as not occurring in a continuing polity, no change will be recognized under the formal theory from the condition sO to the condition $\overline{sO}$ or vice versa.

Assumption 2. No regime change will be recognized as both beginning and ending in the condition $\overline{pM}$, that is, at Level 1. This limitation is adopted to avoid speculative questions. In the absence of bureaucratized defense forces, Level 1 territorial boundaries are readily crossed by armed bands. It is therefore doubtful that the restriction of the theory to events in a continuing polity could be practically maintained for Level 1 conditions. In any case, almost no evidence on Level 1 events has been included in Chapter III.

In a continuing polity there can be no event involving a change in level whereby Level 2 is skipped. In normal circumstances, this presumably follows from the method used to measure level, which is scalar. In normal development or retrogression a polity could hardly fail to pass through the range of values corresponding to any particular level. The present presumption is material rather than formal, however, insofar as it relates to such events as involve a politically induced collapse of social order (and which normally produce radical-egalitarian but occasionally citizen-community regimes) and the subsequent reversion of such a polity to its previous level. In a continuing polity, such a collapse and subsequent restoration of the minimum status order necessary to effective bureaucratic organization can affect no polity more complicated than those at Level 2. At Levels 1 and 2 essential production goes on in autonomic households and is not interrupted by a collapse of the general status order. For a society at a higher level generally to disregard its status order is about as difficult as for a man to stop breathing. It would tend, because of the degree of bureaucratization, materially to interrupt essential production and distribution. In stating a dynamic proposition formally, the subscripts 1 and 2 will be used. Terms in any proposition bearing the subscript 1 refer to a situation immediately preceding a situation referred to by terms in the same proposition bearing the subscript 2.

Hypothesis 4: $\overline{pL_1}$ implies pM_2.

Hypothesis 5: $\overline{pM_1}$ implies pL_2.

The observable consequence of Hypothesis 4 is that an event beginning at Level 3 or Level 4 must be completed at Level 3, 4, or 2, that is, not at Level 1.

The observable consequence of Hypothesis 5 is that an event beginning at Level 1 must be completed at Level 1 (but this is excluded by Assumption 2) or at Level 2.

Except that the formal theory refers only to events in a continuing polity, Hypothesis 4 would be invalidated by the events in Hungary in 1956, wherein a populistic revolutionary upheaval briefly set aside the pre-existing totalitarian regime, since Hungary was at the time at Level 3. The revolutionary regime was classified in Chapter III as a citizen-community because its reaction against a previous Communist regime presumably made Criterion 1 inapplicable, but this regime must have been produced by essentially the same dissolution of the existing status order as normally produces a radical-egalitarian regime. Thus, a Level 3 regime was supplanted by one that the theory presumes to be at Level 1. Technically, there is no invalidation because the change was from a dependent to an independent regime and hence was not an event in a continuing polity. In maintaining Hypothesis 4 and its companion in the face of this event, one must suppose that what happened in Hungary in 1956 was possible only because the existing regime was viewed as a foreign imposition and that otherwise such a total dissolution of the status order as might produce a radical-egalitarian or citizen-community regime in a polity previously bureaucratized to the extent of Level 3 could not occur. In the absence of other similar events, this position still seems reasonable to the present writer.

If not formed at the inception of a polity (as in rebellion, subjection to dependent status, release from dependent status, and the like), a "right" or a "left" within a leadership segment (in the sense of sR or sL) can be created only if the other already exists. Once a leadership segment contains neither a "right" nor a "left" in the sense indicated, it cannot acquire either one in a continuing polity. Exception should be made for a dependent polity since, at least conceivably, the governing power could make a dependent totalitarian regime no longer such and would thereby necessarily re-create a "right" consisting at least of its own representatives if dependency status continued.

Hypothesis 6: $\overline{sO_1}.\ \overline{sR_1}.\ \overline{sL_1}$ implies $\overline{sR_2}.\ \overline{sL_2}$

The verifiable empirical consequence of Hypothesis 6 is that no citizen-community, representative-consensual, totalitarian, or trichotomized without a right regime may change in a continuing polity into a radical-egalitarian regime or into one of the three main-stem regime-types with a right (traditional, dichotomized, trichotomized with a right). This seems rather adequately confirmed by the data in Chapter III.

A leadership segment with tutelary orientation is created

only by the transformation of a "right" or a "left" (in the sense of sR or sL) previously existing by itself in a leadership segment. In other words, if both a "right" and a "left" exist in a leadership segment (as in a traditional or dichotomized regime), one or the other must first be eliminated before the remaining element may constitute itself a totalitarian ruling order. No such limitation would apply in a dependent polity, however, if the ruling power wished to impose a totalitarian regime.

Hypothesis 7: $\overline{sO_1}.\overline{sT_1}.sT_2$ implies $sR_1.\overline{sL_1}$ V $\overline{sR_1}.sL_1$.

The verifiable empirical consequence of Hypothesis 7 is that a totalitarian regime cannot be created in a continuing independent polity except from a radical-egalitarian regime or from a trichotomized regime with a right. (The former origin would necessarily establish a left-wing radical type of imposed ideology like Marxian Communism, while the latter origin would presumably establish a fascistic type of imposed ideology in the totalitarian regime.) Data reported in Chapter III conform to this requirement (the Russian totalitarian regime having been produced from a radical-egalitarian regime, and the Italian and German fascistic regimes having been derived from trichotomized regimes with a right), but such data are scanty because totalitarian regimes do not seem to have existed before World War I and seem rarely to be created in a continuing independent polity. The great majority of known examples were produced in dependent polities under Russian occupation after World War II. A few were formed by rebellion and later, by military action, conquered the territory of a predecessor regime, as in China, Cuba, North Vietnam, Yugoslavia, and Albania. As localized rebelling belligerent regimes, some or all of these may have had initial radical-egalitarian stages.

If a "right" or a "left" or both still exist in a leadership segment, then the regime cannot become managerial without becoming tutelary in orientation, unless the leadership segment is already full-time in character and unless it is reacting to the danger of social and political disruption arising out of the fact that the prevailing popular orientation is leftist.

Hypothesis 8: $\overline{sM_1}.(sR_1 \vee sL_1).sM_2.\overline{sT_2}$ implies $sF_1.pL_1$

The empirical consequence of Hypothesis 8 is a limitation upon the formation of a representative-consensual regime from any regime except a citizen-community, a totalitarian regime, or a trichotomized regime without a right (these regime-types having neither a "right" nor a "left" within their leadership segments). The process of becoming representative-consensual cannot be carried through by a traditional or a radical-egalitarian regime because there is no full-time leadership segment in these regimes. It cannot be carried through by a trichotomized regime with a right because (under the static theory) this regime exists only above Level 2, where the prevailing popular attitude is no longer leftist. Thus, of regimes whose leadership segments contain a "right" or a "left," only a dichotomized regime, because it exists at Level 2 (where the prevailing popular orientation is leftist), can be transformed in a continuing polity into a representative-consensual regime. As with the previous hypothesis, such data as occur in Chapter III relevant to the question confirm this hypothesis, but representative-consensual regimes, like totalitarian regimes, are rarely formed in a continuing polity by the transformation of some other type of regime. Most commonly they are created as the initial regimes in newly liberated polities.

If both a "right" and a "left" exist in a leadership segment, they cannot be simultaneously eliminated except with the adoption by the leadership segment of a managerial orientation.

Hypothesis 9: $sR_1 . sL_1$ implies $sR_2 \vee sL_2 \vee sM_2$.

Aside from eliminating the change from a traditional regime to a citizen-community (already eliminated by Assumption 2) and the change from a traditional regime to a trichotomized regime without a right (already eliminated by Hypothesis 5 together with the static theory), the verifiable empirical consequences of Hypothesis 9 exclude a change from a dichotomized regime to a citizen-community or to a trichotomized regime without a right. There is no conflicting evidence in Chapter III, but it should be noted that no case of a drop from Level 2 to Level 1, such as would be involved in a change from a dichotomized to a citizen-community regime, has been recorded other than the social revolutionary changes that produce a radical-egalitarian regime. It should be noted further that the second requirement would be difficult to refute empirically since one could, under the present criteria, always presume a brief trichotomized regime with a right between a dichotomized regime and a trichotomized regime without a right. A similar difficulty of validation might have been noted for Hypothesis 6, in so far as it bars a reversion from a trichotomized regime without a right to a trichotomized regime with a right. The precise time when a trichotomized regime ceases to have a right cannot be determined under the stated criteria. The present hypothesis, therefore, is perhaps more formal than material. It simplifies the model by eliminating a direct change from a dichotomized regime to a trichotomized regime without a right upon a rise from Level 2 to Level 3.

Once a leadership segment has acquired a managerial

orientation, it will retain this orientation as long as it continues to be full-time in character. Exception must be made for a dependent polity.

Hypothesis 10: $\overline{sO_1}.\, sM_1.\, sF_2$ implies sM_2.

The empirically verifiable consequences of Hypothesis 10 exclude any changes from either a totalitarian or a representative-consensual regime in an independent polity to a dichotomized regime, a trichotomized regime with a right, or a trichotomized regime without a right. Except for the excluded changes to a trichotomized regime without a right, this hypothesis does not add anything to the exclusions of Hypothesis 6. Like the latter hypothesis, it seems to be rather adequately confirmed by the data in Chapter III.

In the case of a totalitarian regime, the leadership segment holds a managerial orientation toward politics, but this is masked by a tutelary orientation under which the leadership segment professes to be applying a definitely promulgated and construed ideology. The continuance of such a tutelary orientation depends upon the utility that the profession of the official ideology appears to hold for the leadership segment. A totalitarian leadership segment has no experience with politics conducted by a leadership segment of managerial orientation without an official ideology, such as occurs in a representative-consensual regime. While the prevailing orientation toward power-wielding in the population is the status orientation, the tutelary leadership segment experiences incipient demands of interest and opinion-groups within the population, but it is largely relieved from the necessity of responding to these demands because insistence upon the official ideology defeats any clear and effective presentation of group positions. Under these conditions, therefore, the leadership segment appears by the profession of an official ideology to be protected from what appears as the prospect of dangerous factional disintegration, which the attitudes of the population seem otherwise likely to bring about within it. Thus, a leadership segment with a tutelary orientation will not abandon that orientation while the status orientation to power-wielding prevails in the population. As with other hypotheses, it appears necessary to make exception for dependent polities. It is also necessary to make exception for the conceivable decline of the socioeconomic level to Level 1, in which case the leadership segment, by ceasing to be full-time in character, would also cease to have a tutelary orientation.

Hypothesis 11: $\overline{sO_1}.\, sT_1.\, pS_2.\, pM_2$ implies sT_2.

The empirically verifiable consequence of Hypothesis 11 is that a totalitarian regime will not cease to be such while it continues at Level 2 or Level 3. This is reasonably well validated by the data of Chapter III, since no totalitarian regime is known to have been transformed into anything else in a continuing polity, but in considering this evidence it should be noted that almost all totalitarian regimes are very recent in origin.

CONSEQUENCES OF THE DYNAMIC THEORY

In the description of an event in a continuing polity the initial situation will be called the "first instance" and the succeeding situation will be called the "second instance." In this chapter Level 4 is not differentiated as a static condition; Levels 3 and 4 are referred to as if constituting one "level." The effect of the dynamic theory just stated on each of the eight independent regime-types, taken as existing in the first instance, is as follows:

1. Citizen-community. This is necessarily at Level 1 under the static theory, and under Assumption 2 and Hypothesis 5 the second instance must be at Level 2. Hypothesis 6 limits the second-instance regime to a representative-consensual, totalitarian, or trichotomized without a right regime. However, the latter under the static theory does not occur at Level 2. Hypothesis 7 eliminates the possibility of a totalitarian regime in the second instance. Thus, the only regime-change in a continuing polity is to a representative-consensual regime at Level 2.

2. Traditional. This is necessarily at Level 1 under the static theory, and under Assumption 2 and Hypothesis 5 the second instance is at Level 2. Hypothesis 7 eliminates a totalitarian regime as the second instance regime. Hypothesis 8 similarly eliminates a representative-consensual regime. The second-instance regime can therefore only be dichotomized.

3. Dichotomized. This is necessarily at Level 2 under the static theory. Hypothesis 7 eliminates the totalitarian as the second instance regime. Hypothesis 9 eliminates the citizen-community and the trichotomized without a right as second-instance regimes. Under the static theory, therefore, the second-instance regime must be traditional or radical-egalitarian at Level 1, representative-consensual at Level 2, or representative-consensual or trichotomized with a right at Level 3 (or 4). Since the exact moment of a change of level cannot be identified empirically, the possibility that the change to a representative-consensual regime might be delayed until the rise from Level 2 to Level 3 will be ignored.

4. Trichotomized with a right. This is necessarily at Level 3 (or 4) under the static theory. Hypothesis 4 limits the second instance to Level 3 (or 4) or Level 2. Hypothesis 8 eliminates the representative-consensual regime as the second-

instance regime. Under the static theory, therefore, the second instance could be a trichotomized regime without a right or a totalitarian regime at Level 3 (or 4), or a dichotomized or totalitarian regime at Level 2. As in the preceding case, the possible change to a totalitarian regime simultaneously with a drop in level will be ignored.

5. Trichotomized without a right. This is necessarily at Level 3 (or 4) under the static theory. Hypothesis 4 limits the second instance to Level 3 (or 4) or Level 2. Hypothesis 6 limits the second instance to a citizen-community (eliminated because at Level 1 under the static theory), a representative-consensual regime, or a totalitarian regime. Hypothesis 7 eliminates the totalitarian regime. Under the static theory, therefore, the second-instance regime can only be representative-consensual, whether at Level 3 (or 4) or at Level 2. As previously, the regime-change at a drop in level will be ignored.

6. Radical-egalitarian. This is treated as at Level 1 under the static theory. Under Assumption 2 and Hypothesis 5 the second instance is at Level 2. Hypothesis 8 eliminates the representative-consensual regime as the second-instance regime. Under the static theory the second-instance regime must therefore be either dichotomized or totalitarian.

7. Totalitarian. This could be at either Level 2 or at Level 3 (or 4) under the static theory. If at Level 3 (or 4), then under Hypothesis 4 the second instance must be at Level 3 (or 4) or at Level 2. Hypothesis 6 eliminates as second-instance regimes the traditional, the radical-egalitarian, the dichotomized and the trichotomized with a right. Hypothesis 10, additionally, eliminates the trichotomized regime without a right. Hypothesis 11 eliminates any regime-change that would be completed at Level 2 or Level 3 (not including Level 4). Although not as yet formally eliminated, the con-

ceivable direct change from Level 2 to Level 4 will be ignored. If the first instance is at Level 2, then under the static theory the second instance can be only a citizen-community at Level 1 or a totalitarian regime at Level 3 (or 4). If the first instance is at Level 3 (or 4), the second instance can be only a totalitarian regime at Level 2 or a representative-consensual regime, but the latter outcome presumes the actual attainment of Level 4.

8. Representative-consensual. This could be at either Level 2 or Level 3 (or 4) under the static theory. If at Level 3 (or 4), then under Hypothesis 4 the second instance must be at Level 3 (or 4) or at Level 2. Hypothesis 6 eliminates all second-instance regimes except the citizen-community, the totalitarian, the representative-consensual, and the trichotomized without a right. Hypothesis 7 eliminates the totalitarian. Hypothesis 10 eliminates the trichotomized without a right. Thus, under the static theory if the first instance is at Level 2, then the second instance can be only a citizen-community at Level 1 or a representative-consensual regime at Level 3 (or 4). If the first instance is at Level 3 (or 4), then no regime-change is possible, though a drop to Level 2 may occur.

The dynamic theory sets no limits on changes among the three possible types of dependent regimes: the dichotomized, the trichotomized, and the totalitarian. However, regime-changes possible under the dynamic theory in a continuing independent polity are limited to those indicated by arrows in Diagram 6.

As can be seen, fifteen types of regime-changes are possible. Five involve a drop in level. None of these are represented by empirical examples in Chapter III except the change from a dichotomized to a radical-egalitarian regime. Five possibilities involve a rise in level. Three of these are represented by specific examples in Chapter III: the reversion from a radical-

Diagram 6. Possible regime-changes in a continuing independent polity

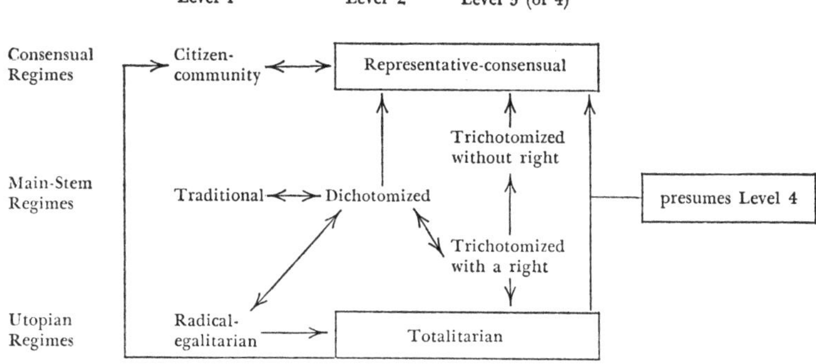

egalitarian to a dichotomized regime, the change from a radical-egalitarian to a totalitarian regime, and the change from a dichotomized regime to a trichotomized regime with a right. The other two are not represented by specific examples. Of the five remaining possibilities, which do not involve any change in level, three are clearly represented: the change from a dichotomized to a representative-consensual regime, that from a trichotomized regime with a right to a totalitarian regime, and that from a trichotomized regime with a right to a trichotomized regime without a right. Two examples, which may possibly have occurred in an continuing independent polity, showing the change from the trichotomized regime without a right to a representative-consensual regime are discussed in Chapter III. No example has been recorded of the change from a totalitarian to a representative-consensual regime.

It will be recalled that the main conclusion reached in Chapter III as to regime-changes in continuing polities was that they are extremely rare. Because this is true, it is not possible to claim that the specifics of the dynamic theory are as fully validated by the data of Chapter III as are the hypotheses of the static theory. However, the dynamic theory here advanced offers a cogent explanation, in terms of the ideas of the model, as to why the rare regime-changes observed empirically were the particular ones they were. In the general lines of the types of regime-changes that the theory excludes, it seems to be rather adequately confirmed by the data of Chapter III.

CHAPTER V

Implications for Africa and Asia

FOR ANY theory of political development, the current question of most salience is the prognosis for the newly liberated countries of Asia and Africa and the few countries on those continents that avoided inclusion in the European colonial empires. Any application of the present theory to these lands must be tentative, since the verification of such application for the past was in respect to nation-states of European cultural antecedents. The polities of Asia and Africa in the middle 1960's are almost all only doubtfully nation-states in the European sense. Many of the new states of Negro Africa contain large areas inhabited by nonliterate tribal peoples. This is also true to a limited extent in Vietnam, India, and other polities of Asia. Even in states where some numerous peoples have acquired an ethnic consciousness, the cultural tolerance of premodern empires has until recently prevailed. The Amharas did not seek to assimilate all other varieties of Ethiopians, nor the Annamese all the peoples of Vietnam. Neither the popular nor the traditional elite cultures of Asian and African countries saw ethnic diversity as incompatible with the existence of a single political state.[1] Modern elite culture, of course, is highly nationalistic

[1]Cf. Rupert Emerson, *From Empire to Nation* (Cambridge, Mass., 1960), p. 128. Edward Shils has said: "The new states of Asia and Africa

in all the non-Western countries, but this sentiment has hardly influenced policy for more than a decade in most of them. Moreover, in spite of the European experience, not much is conclusively known of the process by which a state creates a nationality.[2] Even less can be said of the occasional instances in which a nationality grows up, as in Germany and Italy, before political consolidation is attained.

Much of the literature produced in the last twenty years under the rubric "political development" has been more concerned with national consolidation or integration and similar concepts than with the mechanism of rulership itself. Thus, the treatment in the present book fails almost entirely to make contact with most extant writings on the subject. While the question asked in these pages may be phrased as, "Given a territorial political entity capable of being governed, by what methods can it be ruled?," much of the literature is concerned almost wholly with how a governable territorial political entity of greater than tribal scope may be created. In fact, Edward Shils states: "The central concern of the study of the new states is with the formation of coherent societies and polities."[3] This concern could turn out to be heuristically unprofitable. It leads to much discussion of con-

have not yet reached the point where the people they rule have become nations, more or less coterminous with the state in the territorial boundaries, and possessing a sense of identity in which membership in the state that rules them is an important component." ("On the Comparative Study of the New States" in Clifford Geertz, ed., *Old Societies and New States* [New York, 1963], p. 3).

[2]Clifford Geertz in "The Integrative Revolution: Primordial Sentiments and Civil Politics in the New States," in Geertz, ed., *Old Societies and New States* (New York, 1963), pp. 105–107, urges the study of the processes now going on in the new states for the very reason that earlier instances of the same process left insufficient knowledge.

[3]"On the Comparative Study of the New States" in Geertz, ed., *Old Societies and New States* (New York, 1963), p. 23.

cepts of culture-change and of socialization (as these apply to tribal peoples and to private persons and primary groups in civilization) on the evident assumption that similar processes lead, more or less smoothly, all the way from tribal configuration to nation-state, from personal integration into a "traditional" or "sacred" society to some similar relation of persons to "advanced" or "modern" society, from the social niche occupied by the unobtrusive private person to the area of operation of the executive or ruler. Such an assumption, which tends to confuse the social with the political, the unconscious with the deliberate, the desired with the merely prudently chosen, and ambition with the mere wish for peaceful enjoyment, is very likely unjustified.[4] If, as the model here presented suggests, political structures (and bureaucratic organization in general) are artificial contrivances maintained by the activities of a relatively few clever and assertive persons, they *have to be* taken into account rationally and, within limits, conformed to by the general population to avoid penalization. In this case, politics (and administration in general, whether public or private) will not be much elucidated by concepts designed to deal with family, primary group, or tribal behavior.[5]

[4]Thus, in the most thorough and useful compilation on the developing countries yet produced, Gabriel A. Almond and James S. Coleman, eds., *The Politics of the Developing Areas* (Princeton, 1960), many more sociological and anthropological considerations are presented in the introductory section than manage to get applied seriously in the detailed exposition and the conclusions.

[5]The obscuring of the political—what men deliberately do to, and by the use of, other persons—in modern social thought since the end in 1945 of the biggest political event of all time has certainly been abetted by the almost exclusive concern of personality psychology for the types which Paul Rosenfels in *Psychoanalysis and Civilization* (New York, 1962) describes as yielding or aggressive as against those which he describes as assertive or passive.

These considerations would lead one to suspect that the formation of a coherent polity in a particular place and out of a particular people may be explicable only on an *ad hoc* basis. Some politicians, administrators, generals, and the like, by their more or less intentional and more or less concerted activities, managed (or happened) to bring it about. We do not here flatly assert that there are no explicable organic processes in the growth of nations.[6] We merely submit that it is not known that there are. The present approach to political development, which deals with the governing of a given polity without systematic concern with how the polity itself came to be, could, therefore, turn out to be a valid short cut to the knowledge of political development now widely sought.

Although the present theory has been worked out and tested primarily with reference to nation-states of European culture, this does not mean that it could not be valid for polities that are neither nation-states nor of European antecedents. We only suggest caution against jumping to the conclusion that it applies reliably in such cases. It appears to be applicable. The criteria seem to suffice to classify the polities of Africa and Asia among the eight regime-types. For several of these countries, levels may be computed from available statistics by the preferred method. No obvious, gross invalidations of the theory occur when it is applied to this material, but the evidence is scanty. The formerly colonial countries have histories as independent polities of no more than twenty years at most. Those countries that were not colonies, at least until very recently, were probably at Level 1, and the theory has few verifiable consequences for polities at this low level.

[6]In fact, a very plausible first step in finding such processes has been taken by Karl Deutsch in his *Nationalism and Social Communication* (New York, 1953).

Logically, several possibilities are open. The theory could turn out to be substantially valid as applied to the new non-Western states. It could turn out to be invalid for countries of non-Western culture. This would presumably mean that some of the regularities the theory purports to explain depend, in fact, upon the sharing of some particular beliefs and values among the peoples of Europe, America, and evidently Japan. The theory could also turn out to be invalid for countries that are not nation-states. This would seem to mean that the regularities the theory purports to explain depend in some fashion, which the theory itself does not specify, upon the belonging of political participants to a society having a certain sense of ethnic unity. This seems unlikely, since the substance of the concept "nation" is stretched rather far to include Canada, Belgium, and Switzerland, to whose histories the theory was successfully applied.

More likely than technical invalidity, however, is a somewhat misleading character that may arise in applying the theory to new states while they are as yet in a process of territorial consolidation or disintegration, as some, perhaps most, of them may well be now or in the immediate future. (Even the proportions of this difficulty are not certain. Accidental as are the boundaries of many new polities, there are no rival "historical" boundaries to compare them with. Nations may well form within the present boundaries before the equality in military weakness which now preserves them disappears.) Given territorial flux, however, a prognosis of stability for a representative-consensual regime in a particular country would not technically be invalidated if that country subsequently broke up into several distinct language areas, since such an event is outside the universe of discourse of the formal theory; but if such an outcome occurred, the prognosis of stability might appear to have been misleading.

Similarly, a prognosis for a country of a given area and population might appear quite misleading if subsequent annexations of large neighboring territories had the effect of substantially changing the level or the regime-type or both. This uncertainty as to territorial stability in the new states obviously calls for caution in applying the theory to the "emerging nations," or more particularly in interpreting the results secured from such an application.

As far as levels are concerned, there are few exact data for the new polities of Africa, but somewhat more for those of Asia. Table 6 shows the values for Asian and African countries other than Japan that may be computed from data published in the United Nations *Demographic Yearbook.*

Although, among countries from which data are available, several are rather high on the developmental scale, there is no reason to doubt that most countries of Africa and Asia are at Level 1 or Level 2 or in the intervening range. Thus, they may be expected to have traditional, dichotomized, or totalitarian regimes or if at Level 2 and fortunate in the unity of the native elite at the time of liberation, perhaps representative-consensual. (Modern means of transportation and elementary means of coercion preclude independent polities of the small size and isolated locations necessary for the citizen-community type of regime.)

In those cases in Table 6 showing higher levels, special circumstances seem to be involved. The Israeli population is to a large extent a recent transplant from advanced countries. In general, the status of a commercial entrepot seems to raise the level considerably beyond what it would be on the basis of the local primary and secondary economy taken by itself, as the cases of the United Arab Republic and perhaps Singapore in Table 6 and of Panama among countries considered earlier illustrate. The Singapore case, however, is a curiosity.

Table 6. Levels and relevant values computed for the newly emerging countries*

Countries	Agricultural component (*ag*)	Autonomic component outside agriculture (*ac*)	Decision-audience value (*da*)	Proportion of working force: in manual decision-audience (*mda*)	Proportion of working force: in nonmanual decision-audience (*nmda*)	Level
Pakistan 1951†	76	22	2	0	2	1
Thailand 1947†	84	12	4	0	4	1
South Korea 1955	80	15	5	0	5	1
Thailand 1960	82	11	7	2	5	1–2
Sikkim 1961‡	90	1	9	2	7	1–2
India 1961‡	73	16	11	5	6	2
South Korea 1960‡	65	22	13	4	9	2
Philippines 1960	66	17	17	4	13	2
Syria 1960	60	17	23	9	14	2–3
Taiwan 1956‡	56	19	25	9	16	2–3
Morocco 1960	58	16	26	5	21	2
Iran 1956	54	19	27	11	16	3
United Arab Republic 1960	53	18	29	9	20	2–3
Malaysia 1957	55	16	29	10	19	3
Cyprus 1960	39	24	37	15	22	3
Jordan 1961‡	38	19	43	16	27	3
Israel 1948†	12	37	51	20	31	3–4
Israel 1961‡	14	24	62	24	38	3–4
Singapore 1957	8	29	63	20	43	4

*Except as indicated, data are from Table 13, 1964 number, *Demographic Yearbook*, and values are computed by the preferred methods.

†Data from Table 15, 1956 number, *ibid.*

‡Data from Table 12, 1964 number, *ibid.* Value for *mda* estimated by usual procedure.

Since its separation from Malaysia, Singapore happens to constitute the only instance of a major city at present constituting a polity by itself. Most large modern cities, taken by themselves, are very likely at Level 4. Whether a city-state like Singapore is sufficiently isolated from outside influences to be subject to the normal effects of Level 4 conditions is uncertain.

Application of the criteria to the new countries of Africa and Asia involves some difficulties that are not present where longer and more familiar political histories are available. Collection of data on the spot would seem to be necessary still in the cases of several former colonies less reported upon. On an armchair basis, one can generally determine the applicability of Criterion 1 with a fair degree of certainty. Since there cannot be an "imposed" ideology of the kind intended if there is no seriously developed ideology at all and since some variety of Marxian Communism is about the only ideology already elaborated and available for adoption of any appeal to the underdeveloped countries, one can be reasonably confident that Criterion 1 now applies to those countries ruled by avowed Communist movements and to no others. Thus, at the present time the Soviet Union, mainland China, Mongolia, North Korea, and North Vietnam seem to exhaust the list of polities in Asia and Africa to which Criterion 1 applies. Probably Zanzibar briefly before its absorption into Tanzania came under Criterion 1 and the revolutionary case of Criterion 3, and thus had a radical-egalitarian regime. There seem now to be few cases in which there should be any doubt as to the applicability of Criterion 2, although in the immediate aftermath of World War II there were a good many. Criterion 3, applied on the basis of standard reference material, presents some difficulty in respect to certain countries. Still, one has the strong impression that it is not very commonly applicable in the present-day world. In a few countries like Ethiopia and Afghanistan, Criterion 4 clearly applies. In most present-day polities it obviously does not. There are numerous countries in which recent military coups make it clear that Criterion 5 applies. On the other hand, for the new countries where such coups have not occurred, it is difficult to determine satisfactorily, without much local knowledge, that Criterion 5 does not apply. Probably no such judgment should ordinarily be made with confidence until a couple of decades have elapsed since independence. There was a long period in Pakistan before open military action upset the not too convincing facade of representative constitutional government along British lines which was set up at the time of liberation. Although the level that seems usually to prevail probably makes it an unimportant question, any firm determination as to whether or not Criterion 6 applies would usually require somewhat intimate local knowledge of a polity. In most cases where the question is relevant, rationalist-institutionalist (i.e., leftist) and traditionalist-personalist (i.e., rightist) thinking seem to constitute clearly contrasting viewpoints at the elite level, making Criterion 7 applicable, but there are exceptions like Iran where the clear differentiation of a radical-egalitarian left seems to indicate a trichotomized regime.

Although no attempt will be made at a detailed classification of individual regimes in Africa and Asia, some summary findings seem fairly clear. None of the countries of Asia and Africa, except China and some on the peripheries of China, are as yet totalitarian. Most of the polities in these countries presumably have dichotomized or traditional regimes, the latter mostly in Africa or Arabia. A few have trichotomized regimes with a right. In all probability, there are several countries where the organization, political experience, and sensed unity of the native elite at the time of independence created representative-consensual regimes, but it is difficult to be fully confident of the individual cases in which this occurred without on-the-spot knowledge. Likely candidates for this classification are India, Malaya, Tunisia, and Tanzania.

There seems, therefore, to be a good chance that if the

present theoretical scheme becomes familiar to enough persons closely acquainted with the newly emerging countries, it will be found valid and relevant in relation to them. If this does occur, it will call for some rather marked changes in viewpoint toward underdeveloped countries on the part of policy-makers and experts in the developed countries.

The present theory is totally in conflict with the view now widely held among experts and policy-makers in the United States that the establishment of stable and effective democratic regimes in those underdeveloped countries that at present lack them is attainable on a gradual and incremental basis and will be facilitated by success in the attainment of higher levels of economic production.[7] The difficulty with this view, in the light of the theory here developed, is that it confuses an abstract quality, democracy, which may be inherent in greater or lesser degree in a governmental system, with the governmental system itself. Except possibly for some variants of the citizen-community at Level 1, there is no institutional pattern of rulership that can realistically be called democracy. A representative-consensual regime (a form of government) may be more or less democratic (i.e., open to influences, claims, and pressures originating in all parts of its population) or oligarchic (i.e., responding only to influences from a narrowly defined portion of its population). In degree, the same is true of a totalitarian regime, although the effect of a uniform, prescribed ideology is to block the effective expression of most claims arising outside the ruling elite, and hence the degree of democracy could hardly be

[7]The most thorough scholarly version of what appears to be the official United States viewpoint on how to deal with the underdeveloped countries is probably Max F. Millikan and Donald L. M. Blackmer, eds., *The Emerging Nations: Their Growth and United States Policy* (Boston and Toronto, 1961).

very high. Nonetheless, the government of the Soviet Union is relatively more democratic than was that of Hitler's Germany. Equally, main-stem regimes may be more or less democratic, and their instability means that often in the same country the degree of democracy varies from high to very low over a very short period. In fact, at Level 2, as long as the main-stem condition persists, the most that one can expect is an occasional "here today, gone tomorrow" sample of democratic practice.

By treating democracy as a form of government, which in large countries and countries at all urbanized it is not, the prevailing view entirely conceals the nature of the problem of institutional stability, which is the central problem of political development for most countries now underdeveloped. Merely attempting to promote democratic values in underdeveloped main-stem countries by encouraging egalitarian tendencies and by disparaging the privileges of the well-to-do, which in the realm of strictly *political* development seems to be the actual scope of United States policy in the underdeveloped countries, contributes nothing to institutional stability and very likely works in the contrary direction.

Under the theory developed in this book, the attainment of institutional stability is a clear-cut and definite event and has nothing whatever to do with the gradual extension of democratic or egalitarian values. Stability is attained in a previously main-stem polity at Level 2 only by the full and complete substitution of a totalitarian or representative-consensual regime. In the case of a totalitarian regime, this could be the outcome of organized civil war in which the totalitarian regime, established by rebellion or invasion in some pocket of the territory of the polity, expands militarily and conquers the entire area. The other possible origin of a totalitarian regime—historically rare, since it is dependent upon the wholesale subversion of rank-and-file troops or police—is from a radical-egalitarian regime that is the product of the fairly sudden collapse of the previous status-order (and its props in the policing system) throughout most or all of the territory of the polity. Although the establishment of a representative-consensual regime by the military success of a belligerent in civil war is not theoretically impossible, it is practically so in countries that do not already have a long tradition of effective representative government, at least in local matters.

A deliberate coming-together of rival factions of the political elite under a sort of nonaggression pact seems to be the only ordinarily practical way of establishing a representative-consensual regime at Level 2. Such an arrangement would have to be motivated by a fear of the possible alternative, a left-wing totalitarian take-over. Hence, the leadership segment so established would tend to include rather conservative personnel, and the arrangement would have to offer some assurance of protecting their interests. In fact, all interests that are to remain influential after the settlement have to be included, and any tendency in the arrangements to exclude too many influential persons (necessarily by rather drastic means, the least severe of which would be exile) would defeat the project by undermining the trust of the remainder of the participants. Thus, the process by which a representative-consensual regime could be established at Level 2 is likely to be an uncongenial one for persons of radical, liberal, or dogmatically democratic views.

At Level 3, which some of the underdeveloped countries have attained, the possibilities of stabilizing previously mainstem polities are substantially different. This is largely because bureaucratic organizations, including the means of policing, have expanded considerably. Though main-stem regimes with a right continue unstable, there is no longer a possibility of a sudden collapse of the status-order producing a radical-egalitarian regime. It is still possible, however, that a left-wing totalitarian belligerent with a territorial foothold might prevail over the previous regime by military operations. It is also possible that the regime will transform itself into a right-wing totalitarian regime. This seems unlikely. The motivation in previous instances (Italy and Germany) rested strongly upon an appraisal of possibilities as being essentially those of Level 2. Most Level 3 political elites are probably now aware of the more conservative public that Level 3 conditions produce.

A "settlement," bringing together all elite interests to transform a main-stem regime into a representative-consensual one, is no longer possible at Level 3. Elites are now too large. It would be impossible to carry along all the organized followings of the major leaders. Instead, stability may be attained at Level 3 by the change from a trichotomized regime with a right to a trichotomized regime without a right. This is made possible by the fact that at Level 3 a majority of the population is aware that it is not at the bottom of the social pyramid and that it has some status or privilege to lose in any general social equalization. Hence, a stable popular majority is available to support a suitable political vehicle—conservative but not narrowly aristocratic or plutocratic, populistic in tone but without the suggestion of blue-collar egalitarianism. If such a political vehicle—a "centrist" party—can be created, it can be counted upon continuously to win elections against the opposition of a large but minority egalitarian trend, principally centered in the manual decision-audience. It is the *demonstration* that this can be done, perhaps through several elections over a protracted period of time, that brings about the abdication and dissolution of the "right," usually by then only a *de facto* right comprising mainly the upper military command. Through its greater legitimacy, particularly in the view of the egalitarians who are feared, a representative government based on democratic suffrage, if it can be counted upon to be socially conservative, offers more security to those who fear social experiments than does a tendency to rely crudely on military interventions in politics. While, as the experiences of the last few years in Argentina indicate, it is sometimes very difficult to arrange suitable partisan vehicles for a demonstration, sooner or later political shrewdness is likely to accomplish it. Over the next few decades we may anticipate that a good many Level 3 main-stem regimes will stabilize themselves in this fashion.

Although the theory as developed in Chapter IV shows the added possibility even at Level 3 of a further transition from a trichotomized without a right to a representative-consensual regime, it seems that such a change can be accomplished only as the conditions of Level 4 are reached. Between the constantly winning center and the constantly losing egalitarian left in a trichotomized regime without a right, deep (and occasionally violent) ideological conflict tends to persist until, with the increase of the nonmanual decision-audience to a very large fraction of the population, the bases for ideological distinctions become blurred in the population as a whole. Until then the leadership segment, consisting essentially of the centrist leadership, remains on the defensive psychologically and does not acquire a fully managerial view of politics.

CHAPTER VI

The Future of the Highly Developed Countries

WHATEVER MAY be the case with the newly emerging countries, there is no question that development (in the sense of the increase of the decision-audience, and particularly of the nonmanual decision-audience, as a percentage of the working force) is occurring today in the countries that have already reached rather high levels in Europe and in the countries of European cultural antecedents.[1] Well before the end of this century, Western Europe (with the possible excep-

[1]Our study is limited to political development. We have taken socio-economic development as a datum. The belief, mainly attributable to the writings of W. W. Rostow, especially *The Stages of Economic Growth* (Cambridge, 1960), that the economy of a country is either reliably self-sustaining in "growth," or is not, appears to be widely accepted by those competent to judge. Rostow's stages do not correlate closely with our levels. If the dates of changes in concrete cases given by Rostow are compared with our data in Chapter II, it appears that development, possibly even to Level 4, may occur without "take-off." The change from Level 1 to Level 2 probably must precede take-off. Take-off is most likely to occur at the transition from Level 2 to Level 3. Perhaps it would occur naturally at this point in a completely isolated economy. In appraising the prospects for development of the under-developed countries, we have been influenced by William Frederick Cottrell, *Energy and Society* (New York, 1955), though we are open-minded as to the truth of his thesis that only the countries now highly developed are likely to be able to develop.

tion of Spain and Portugal) and the countries of English speech and culture in other parts of the world will all be at Level 4 and will have reached, or be closely approaching, the point where, logically, "development," as measured by the standards used in this book, must cease. In reaching total or almost total bureaucratization, these populations will have attained a form of social organization quite without historical precedent before the present century and—a somewhat more disquieting fact—a form of social organization quite unforeseen by the human imagination, certainly unforeseen by those who proposed reforms and advanced utopias.[2]

That the advanced societies of the late twentieth century will live in a social world that nobody wanted is a function of the trick social equalization played upon its advocates and promoters. In retrospect, it seems fairly clear that in concrete actions, traditionalists tried unsuccessfully to maintain inequality of family status and that liberals and radicals successfully undermined it in the social struggles of recent centuries. However, *pari passu,* with the undermining of the inequalities of families, modern social development increased the unequal status of individual persons in the serious activities of daily living, where in the past most persons were fairly equal if unimportant participants. In the leisures and diversions of life in the advanced countries, equality is rapidly spreading because these countries are so productive that few persons have to work very long or very hard and it is relatively easy to allow a high average income level. On the other hand, responsible, influential, and creative activities become

[2]For a European view of the current bureaucratization of society and how technical and social progress make it much more acceptable than might have been supposed, see Michel Crozier, "La burocrazia come sistema di organizzazione," *Tempi moderni,* Anno V, Gruppo IV (1962), 93–116.

more and more demanding on the individual persons who are able to participate in them. Ambitious persons seek to work evenings and weekends, while others disport themselves, in order to assure that they may be indispensable participants in decision-making that depends on esoteric knowledge or at least on full-time attention. Though a formal dependence of public authority on mass suffrage is universal in the very highly developed countries today, it is more difficult than in the past to speak of popular decision-making. Regular elections, on a nation-wide basis at least, become measures of mood and morale, to be taken into account by decision-makers in alloting domestic income and in undertaking expensive or dangerous foreign commitments.

Two consequences, one in political institutions and the other in the development of political culture, appear to inhere in the attainment of Level 4. The first, the exclusion of all political forms that depend upon ideologies—social-class-oriented political belief systems—calls for an elaboration of the formal theory developed in Chapter IV. It will be the subject of the next section of the exposition. The other, an elaboration of political culture to embrace what in the past were the esoterics of rulership, will be discussed in general terms in the concluding section of this chapter.

THE THEORY EXTENDED TO DIFFERENTIATE LEVEL 4

In Chapter IV a model centered upon possible elite and mass attitudes toward power-wielding was presented. In terms of the concepts of this model, eleven hypotheses and certain nonempirical assumptions were advanced to express a theory of essentially three levels of political development (Level 4 being subsumed in Level 3 for most purposes). This theory was rather adequately validated by the accumulated evidence as to nation-states of European antecedents set forth in Chapter III. The theory in Chapter IV was not extended to differentiate Level 4 because historical evidence does not as yet fully confirm what it appears necessary, in terms of the model, to postulate.

It will be recalled that in developing the model it was pointed out that the managerial attitude to power-wielding is strictly incompatible with fixed doctrines as to the proprieties of social stratification, that the managerial attitude tends in attenuated form to extend through the nonmanual decision-audience, and that the size attained by the nonmanual decision-audience at Level 4 (given any reasonable assumption as to social mobility) ensures that practically all families will be influenced by the managerial attitude at the same time that the affluence which high productivity affords at Level 4 removes from the masses any interest in elaborating defensive or offensive idea-systems around their working situation. Thus, the managerial attitude, always prevalent among elites, may at Level 4 be rather freely expressed publicly since it no longer, as at lower levels, conflicts with widely held popular attitudes.

Therefore, in an independent polity when the status orientation toward power-wielding no longer prevails in the population, the leadership segment will necessarily take a managerial attitude toward politics.

Hypothesis 12: $s\overline{O}.\ \overline{pS}$ implies sM.

The observable consequence of this hypothesis is to exclude main-stem regime-types (in which the managerial attitude to politics is not characteristic of the leadership segment) at Level 4.

However, the tutelary attitude characteristic of the leadership segment of a totalitarian regime also involves a form of class-oriented ideology. More important, it is maintained by the essentially managerially oriented leadership segment as a protection against the need to respond to status-oriented political positions emanating from the masses. If such positions are no longer seriously involved in mass sentiments, as is true at Level 4, the motivation for the totalitarian leadership to retain its tutelary orientation could not survive in an independent polity at Level 4.

Hypothesis 13: $\overline{sO}.\, sT$ implies pS.

The observable effect of this hypothesis is to eliminate the totalitarian regime-type at Level 4.

Differentiating Level 4 on the basis of the foregoing two hypotheses allows the expansion of Diagram 5, on p. 200, which summarizes the static theory, into the form seen in Diagram 7.

Diagram 7. Summary of static theory, differentiating Level 4

	Level 1	Level 2	Level 3	Level 4
States of population	$\overline{pM}\cdot$ $pS\cdot$ pL	$pM\cdot$ $pS\cdot$ pL	$pM\cdot$ $pS\cdot$ $\overline{pL}$	$pM\cdot$ $\overline{pS}\cdot$ $\overline{pL}$
Consequent limitations on states of leadership segments	$\overline{sF}$	$sF\cdot$ $(sL$ $\vee$ $sM)$	$sF\cdot$ $\overline{sL}$	$sF\cdot$ $\overline{sL}\cdot$ $sM\cdot$ $\overline{sT}$

The first two columns, representing Levels 1 and 2, remain as in Chapter IV. For the second two columns, taken from the third column of Diagram 5, a full-time leadership segment and the absence of a "left" within the leadership segment continue to be required. In addition, in the last column, referring to Level 4, the leadership segment must have a managerial but not a tutelary orientation. In other words, at

Level 4 only the representative-consensual regime is viable.

It will be recalled that the actual findings reported in Chapter III conform to this requirement. However, only regimes already representative-consensual before they reached Level 4 in a continuing polity (with the possible exceptions of Norway and Denmark) have as yet been recorded at Level 4. Thus, the crucial test of Hypotheses 12 and 13, the change of a regime from main-stem or totalitarian to representative-consensual in a continuing polity during the transition from Level 3 to Level 4 has as yet not been certainly observed. One place to watch for such a development would seem to be Czechoslovakia, at present a totalitarian regime but already at a high level of development.

In judging this feature of the theory against future evidence one must note that although the representative-consensual regime in the present model includes all stable cases of democratic representative government, it is not necessarily a democratic regime. All that is required for a representative-consensual regime is institutional stability in a bureaucratized regime without a single imposed ideology. Thus, a totalitarian regime would become representative-consensual if divergent political positions came to be publicly expressed by prominent leaders, even if effective control of policy continued to be confined to a restricted body such as the present ruling Communist party. Similarly, a main-stem regime would become representative-consensual once all the criteria (but especially Criteria 4, 5, and 6) ceased to apply, even though full democratic participation in the right of suffrage was not attained.

To complete the dynamic theory, it must be noted that main-stem attitudes appear to be maintained in a leadership segment at Level 3 even after there is no "right" or "left" within the leadership segment while there is a prevailing popular status-orientation to power-wielding. Thus, the transition to a managerial but not tutelary orientation in the leadership segment cannot be completed except (as has been indicated in Hypothesis 8) while under the threat of social revolutionary upheaval because the prevailing popular orientation to power-wielding is leftist or else when the popular attitude to power-wielding is no longer status-oriented.

Hypothesis 14: $\overline{sM_1}.\, sM_2.\, \overline{sT_2}$ implies $pL_2 \vee \overline{pS_2}$.

The empirical consequence of Hypothesis 14 is that a trichotomized regime without a right would continue as such and would not become representative-consensual as long as the polity remained at Level 3.

Diagram 6 on p. 215, summarizing the dynamic theory, may be restated as in Diagram 8 to take account of Hypotheses 12, 13, and 14 and to differentiate Level 4 from Level 3.

THE ELABORATION OF POLITICAL CULTURE TO EMBRACE MANAGERIAL BEHAVIOR

The proliferation of large-scale bureaucratic organizations in modern society has made conspicuous the routine operations of powerful persons. This circumstance makes visible today aspects of personal power that were present but less easy to see in past history. A really powerful person in an organized context necessarily tends to become so totally occupied with the shrewd and expedient exercise of his power that he can make few decisions on considerations other than those which relate to preserving the organizational situation where his exercise of power is effective. In effect, he must seek to restrain the actions of those over whom he has power in such ways as to prevent the development of conflicting motivations within his human environment to the point where the latter would be unmanageable. Roughly, if the deference

Diagram 8. Possible regime-changes in a continuing independent polity with Level 4 differentiated

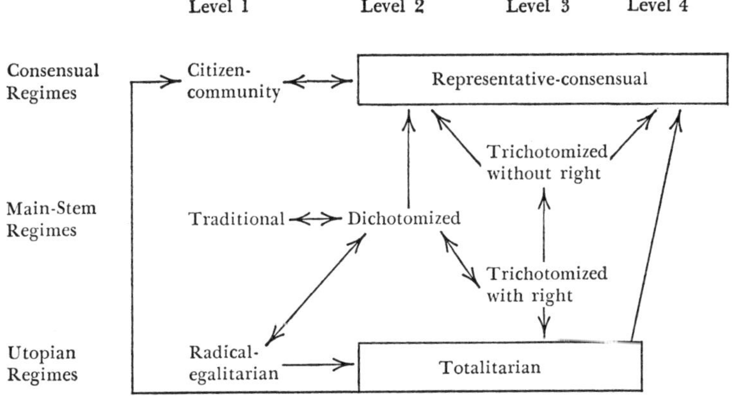

or at least the quietude of B, C, D (where—depending on the context—B, C, D may be individual persons or groupings of persons) is necessary to the power of A (A—depending on the context—being either an individual person or some organization), then, in order to maintain his power, A must forestall all situations where, because of sufficiently developed hostile inclinations among B, C, D, he would have to choose to act with less than an overwhelming portion of B, C, D against the remainder. Managerial behavior, therefore, is the behavior of persons possessing power that aims at suppressing incipient conflicts which, if developed, would reduce their power. In practice, managerial behavior tends to preserve such organized social contexts as exist, but the complexities of actual organizations and the impossibility of always finding an expedient managerial course of action prevents managerial behavior from making actual organizations immortal.

In a revised orientation toward history, the concept of managerial behavior could substitute in part for the motivations usually imputed to dominant interests, ruling classes, and similar entities in which individual powerful persons are seen only as parts of broader culture groups. Aside from such cultural settings, which of course affect the motivations of powerful persons, personal power universally defines an interest and hence a set of motivations irrespective of the cultural setting. The behavior of powerful persons motivated by the mere fact of the possession of power, moreover, is the essential and necessary mechanism on which all perdurant social organization beyond intimate family-type groups depends. There is nothing else that suffices to prevent the differing motivations which necessarily arise among participants in any complex organized context from more or less rapidly disrupting any possibility of co-operation. Formal and impersonal organization persists as the result of the successful manipulation of incipient conflicts by those persons possessing sufficient power to be interested in keeping the situation manageable.

Most powerful persons in earlier societies were not as busy at the task of power-wielding as are bureaucratic executives today. The managerial aspect of their behavior was relatively moderate, and doubtless, they made many decisions because of cultural or ideological presumptions or merely to satisfy personal impulses. In the area of political rulership, however, in any society with significant bureaucratic organization—that is, in any society at a level above Level 1—real power can never be held without full-time attention to its exertion. Thus, the politically powerful in such societies have been in a situation conducive to a considerable degree of managerially oriented behavior.

Although the behavior of powerful persons at levels above Level 1 has tended to a considerable degree to be managerially oriented, below Level 4 such behavior has had to be justified and rationalized in terms of the status-orientation to power-wielding that prevailed within the general population.

Deliberately propagated ideologies as well as customary political culture at Levels 2 and 3 (where most recorded history has occurred) have, therefore, always had a somewhat misleading character. They have expressed the public preconceptions as to what politics is all about and have in broad terms limited the behavior of powerful persons by limiting the available justifications for such behavior, but they have also often distracted attention from the motivations of powerful persons on the basis of which specific political decisions were taken.

The attainment of Level 4 in important countries of the world has tended to dissolve customary political viewpoints, because these viewpoints reflected the status-orientation to power-wielding that no longer prevails in populations at Level 4. Viewing the wielding of power in managerial terms no longer at Level 4 belongs strictly to the *arcana imperii,* the mysteries of power. It is widely possible at Level 4 for ordinary persons to see politics in managerial terms because, with the proliferation of bureaucratic organization, many persons are themselves seriously engaged in the exercise of power (at least on a small scale) and most persons are intimately acquainted with people who are so engaged.

If power-wielding tends to be managerial whenever the power-wielder is strictly absorbed in this activity, and if the traditional viewpoints that have made this fact a secret of the powerful are dissolved in polities at Level 4, politics may be expected to evolve along wholly unprecedented lines in polities that reach Level 4 and perhaps to a considerable extent on a world-wide scale because of the cultural influence such countries will exert. Anomie is currently noticeable among youth generally in many of the more advanced countries and within privileged circles influenced by world-wide cultural trends in less developed lands. This mood resembles that often found in the past among some offspring of the well-to-do. It is a clear reflection of the loss of meaning of a large part of traditional social wisdom, which reflected the status-orientation to power-wielding. Given both affluence (and the resultant indulgence of society toward the deviant and the "unmotivated") and the constant deliberate manipulation of the behavior of persons by other persons—features never pervading whole societies in the past—the rethinking of a realistic social morality will be difficult but should not unduly tax human ingenuity in the next generation or so. The problem is already defined, and the time is available to think it out. Contrary to a widespread assumption, the advanced countries are not facing a future of persisting social change. In all the concrete meaning that "social change" has ever carried, they have already had about all there is of it to have. "Social change" has always referred to the consequences of the growth (and perhaps occasionally the temporary decline) of the decision-audience as a proportion of the working force. It is the process by which more and more ordinary people have come to live in a social environment characterized by the constant conscious wielding of power that has hitherto always been the social environment of high elites. In this sense, social change was a process of democratization.

The prospect in Level 4 polities (and possibly in a world widely influenced by such societies) for the general values of Western democratic culture is not a dark one, in spite of the disvaluation of the connotations of the word "power" in the traditional expressions of this culture. An intellectual clarification of social relations may be expected, once the double bookkeeping by which powerful persons accounted to themselves individually and to their publics collectively for their actions may be dispensed with. The legitimate function of the power of individual persons will be clearly seen for what it is (and what tends to become its actual function when the power-wielder is sufficiently specialized as such)—a necessary and effective mechanism for preserving social peace. The abuse of power—its use in place of legitimate influence based on other considerations to determine the lines of technical, aesthetic, and philosophic development—may the more easily be curbed, once the legitimate need for power to restrain behavior tending toward conflict is clearly recognized. If power is seen to have a clear and legitimate purpose (which it has never had in traditional democratic thought), it may the more readily be held to that purpose. One may expect a much greater development than past history has foreshadowed of the possibility of convincing persons rationally with regard to what policies are needed and what are not. For the advanced countries, if they existed in a world by themselves, the "role of management in history" would suggest a benign future.[3]

[3]We are unimpressed by the crudities frequently attributed to the "organizational man" as a type. He could hardly function smoothly in a role—the wielding of discrete snippets of power—for which there is as yet no accepted cultural tradition. Our most notable impression from William H. Whyte, Jr.'s so far definitive study of the new American bureaucratic type, *The Organizational Man* (Garden City, N.Y., 1956), is of dynamic social groupings within which many more individual persons are obviously asserting themselves effectively than could have been true in any but high elite circles in the past. The nostalgia for the autonomic disguise normally worn by the enterpriser and innovator of the past century produces a tendency to see organizational life under the rubrics of psychopathology; see for instance, Robert Presthus, *The Organizational Society* (New York, 1962). We would say merely that the new bureaucrats are ordinary people living in a social environment like that in which high elites always lived without an excessive incidence of mental disease. Except in a few favored environments where land was plentiful and aristocrats scarce, the autonomic has been the one whose trivial range of concerns and lack of concepts adequate for viewing the social world about him caused him to run the greater risk of mental crippling.

Index

DATE DUE
